By the author of *Decoding Doomsday*

Black Sun, Blood Moon

Can We Escape the Cataclysms of the Last Days?

Foreword by
Dr. Thomas R. Horn

S. Douglas Woodward

Also by S. Douglas Woodward

ARE WE LIVING IN THE LAST DAYS?
The Apocalypse Debate in the 21st Century

DECODING DOOMSDAY:
The 2012 Prophecies, the Apocalypse and
the Perilous Days Ahead

Contributing author to:
PANDEMONIUM'S ENGINE
Edited by Thomas R. Horn

Black Sun, Blood Moon

Can We Escape the Cataclysms of the Last Days?

*"And I beheld when he had opened the sixth seal, and, lo,
there was a great earthquake; and
the sun became black as sackcloth of hair,
and the moon became as blood."*
Revelation 6:12

S. Douglas Woodward

Defender Publishing Group
Crane, MO.

Black Sun, Blood Moon

Can We Escape the Cataclysms of the Last Days?

Defender Publishing LLC, Crane, MO.
www.defenderpublishing.com

Printed in the United States of America in 2011.

Scripture taken from the King James Version of the Bible unless otherwise noted.

All photographs of artwork used in this book or on the cover are public domain and taken from Microsoft 'clip art' or the Wikimedia JPEG 'Commons' unless otherwise noted.

To order multiple copies of the book, please mail info@faith-happens.com.

For information on the author, please see www.faith-happens.com.

For additional information on this book, see www.blacksunbloodmoonbook.com.

Prophecy/ 2012 / Eschatology

ISBN-10: 0984630066

ISBN-13: 9780984630066

Cover design by the author.

Black Sun, Blood Moon

Table of Contents

Acknowledgements

This book is dedicated to my father, William C. Woodward, who remains a steadfast example of true spirituality, unconditional Christian love, and attentive commitment to his family... all at 91 years young!

* * * * *

Special thanks to everyone I've solicited to provide comments, raise questions, and gain ideas for titles, cover design, and appropriateness of content. I remain, however, solely responsible for any and all mistakes contained within this work.

Thanks to Tom Horn for his terrific *Foreword* and support during the publication of this book.

As always, thanks to my wonderful wife Donna, for her enduring love and support during the time I've been missing in action preparing this manuscript for publication.

Black Sun, Blood Moon

Black Sun, Blood Moon

FOREWORD
Dr. Thomas R. Horn

A couple years back we received a manuscript at Defender Publishing House with the title *Decoding Doomsday*, by S. Douglas Woodward. I do not recall exactly why we initially turned down the opportunity to publish it, but later we corrected that huge mistake and today are excited to distribute it as well as the new triumphant work you hold in your hands – ***Black Sun, Blood Moon: Can We Escape the Cataclysms of the Last Days?***

You are about to discover what changed our minds on Woodward, as he handily carves out a deeper niche toward becoming one of the most prolific and critical thinkers on apocalyptic themes, historical-eschatological scholarship, and its in-depth analysis today. Like Orson Welles so famously promised during the 1970s marketing slogan for Paul Masson Winery, "We will sell no wine before its time," Woodward seems incapable of rushing past facts and opinions without first carefully selecting, researching, and annotating those materials to verify their veracity and to wring out of them riveting, unexpected delights.

Despite this attention to detail, his writing style is both easy and enjoyable, making complex topics plain while simultaneously offering astonishing new, 'page turning' discoveries one after another. His insights emanate from a studied, in-depth Pre-millennial point of view – without the slightest trace of dogmatism – demonstrating an especially keen knowledge of the Bible. Each chapter builds upon the previous, from crescendo to crescendo, culminating in captivating as well as hermeneutically sound conclusions.

Such a writer, dedicating himself in his first three books to the topic of prophecy, is perfect for the times in which we live. Much of the world feels as if it is now falling apart as we witness banking/economic conspiracies, unproven and perhaps dangerous new technologies, frightening developments in nature, and astounding 'signs in the heavens.' Recent polls show that a majority of Christians, especially evangelicals, believe current upheavals are indications from God that the 'end of days' draws near. Many folk in our society today – not just the 'religious' – look for learned leaders who can communicate, to aid their understanding of the cryptic prophetic books of the Bible and what they foretell for the times just ahead. Woodward is that man. Having studied the subject of eschatology for over 40 years, he is in a unique position to offer fresh ways of expounding on what the Bible teaches (as well as correcting many decades old mistakes evident in some traditional interpretations of prophetic subject matter).

For instance, in Chapter 12, Doug directs our attention toward the identity of Antichrist and answers the question why, though the Bible nowhere directs us to keep watch for the "Man of Sin," we just can't seem to help ourselves. Among other factors, current global events suggest the time is right for a man of superior intelligence, wit, charm, and diplomacy to emerge on the world scene as our savior. But behind this personage, so we learn, will be a profound comprehension and irresistible presence resulting from a supersensible 'mind' of collective knowledge, at least 5,000 years in the making. This remarkable being will be the embodiment of a very old, super-intelligent spirit worshipped in ancient Sumeria, Babylon, Egypt, Greece, and Rome. Just as Jesus Christ was the "seed of the woman" (Genesis 3:15), Antichrist will be the "seed of the serpent." So then, how can the Antichrist also be of Greek, Roman, and Jewish genealogy as foretold by the Prophet Daniel? Woodward enlightens us. Moreover, although foretold by numerous Scriptures and facetiously discussed in modern entertainment, the world at large will not recognize him for what he actually is – paganism's evil facsimile to God's incarnation in Jesus Christ – the "Beast" of Revelation 13:1.

After possessing a man of distinguished character, the ancient spirit within Antichrist ultimately transforms him into "a king of fierce countenance" (Daniel 8:23). With imperious decree, he facilitates a 'one-world government,' universal religion, and through his 'mark,' global economic socialism. Ultimately, he exalts himself *"above all that is called God, or that is worshiped, so that he, as God, sitteth in the temple of God, showing himself that he is God"* (2 Thessalonians 2:4).

But **Black Sun, Blood Moon** covers far more than the identity of the Antichrist. My mention of this topic is little more than a tease for the in-depth and startling facts Woodward unearths chapter after chapter. The author also provides provocative and fresh insights in many other areas:

- The world's fascination with the year 2012 and its link to the apocalypse of the Bible.
- The legitimacy behind the 2012 forecasts for natural disasters, solar storms, hurricanes, tsunamis, and cataclysmic earthquakes such as hit Japan in March, 2011.
- The possibility that Christians can escape the massive cataclysms determined for the period of time the Bible calls, *The Great Tribulation:*
  - ✓ Comets that threaten to strike earth with deadly force;
  - ✓ Cauldrons like Yellowstone Park which could explode, sending mountains of volcanic ash into the atmosphere, and
  - ✓ Plagues unleashed through bio-terrorism or genetic tampering.
- Date-setting attempts to predict the timing of these events.

- What the Bible teaches about the nature of the world's creation and its implications for the new world to come.
- How 'doomsday' speaks to humanity's quest for meaning.
- The biblical depictions of the world AFTER Armageddon.
- The nature of immortality and the Bible's teaching regarding the afterlife.
- And much more.

To be perfectly clear: Woodward's book isn't a litany of gloomy facts. At the core of almost every topic is a premise of hope, both for today and the future. That's why readers will not only learn a great number of new things on the topics Woodward tackles (the reading light will burn late into the night), they will be encouraged for having done so. Indeed, the structure of the book lends itself to contemplative consideration of the material and even small group discussion. It is a most unusual volume.

After reading **Black Sun, Blood Moon** you may become, as I have, a fan of S. Douglas Woodward. We are indebted to this thoughtful researcher and writer for the vast amount of energy and investigation so obvious in this new book.

Dr. Thomas R. Horn, President
Defender Publishing LLC

April, 2011

INTRODUCTION:
Is the Apocalypse Avoidable?

*And I beheld when he had opened the sixth seal, and, lo, there was a
great earthquake; and the sun became black as sackcloth of hair, and
the moon became as blood.* (Revelation 6:12)

*[Jesus] answered and said unto them, "When it is evening, ye say, 'It
will be fair weather: for the sky is red.' And in the morning, 'It will be
foul weather today: for the sky is red and lowering.' O ye hypocrites, ye
can discern the face of the sky; but can ye not
discern the signs of the times?" (Matthew 16:2, 3)*

THERE IS AN OLD SAYING — RED SKY AT NIGHT — SAILORS DELIGHT. RED SKY IN THE MORNING — SAILORS TAKE WARNING!

The weatherman says this rule of thumb applies only to the middle latitudes of our planet. The evening sky of red represents an abundance of tiny particles in the atmosphere, typical of a high pressure system. It yields clear skies overhead. On the other hand, a red sky in the morning bears bad tidings because it implies a storm is approaching, particularly if the sky is lowering at the same time.

Jesus' adage was the equivalent Hebrew aphorism. The point Jesus made was how paradoxical that the religious leaders of the day could tell the weather (not their expertise) while failing to foresee how the religious and political climate would affect their nation — matters about which they were supposed experts. It was a giant case of not seeing the forest for the trees. The Jewish leadership should have recognized that cataclysm was inevitable. All the ingredients were there, like chemicals ready to combust.

However, this leadership had a stake in keeping the status quo. Hoping against hope, the Pharisees and Sadducees compromised aspects of their sovereignty to maintain their tenuous hold on the religion of the Jewish people. Enjoying a separation of church and state (of sorts), they accepted Rome as the keepers of the order, while priests practiced the Mosaic Law unperturbed. Their fatal mistake was assuming that 'church and state' could remain so neatly distinct allowing the negotiated peace accord to last indefinitely.

Without question, Jesus' day was a time when fervent Jewish nationalism butted against Roman hegemony. Zealots, the freedom fighters of their day, continued to test the resolve of their Roman occupiers. Insurrection never seemed more than one incident away. As we know, Jesus would be a victim of this tense atmosphere. He was crucified to temporarily quench the fire fueling Hebrew revolt. Despite the fact that Jesus' solution – inward transformation – could have quieted the tempest fanning these flames of rebellion, both Romans and Jews saw fit to crucify Him instead, during the quiet morning hours before the multitude awakened. The leadership of both factions feared that the agitated throng – drawn to Jerusalem for the momentous Jewish holy day, Passover – would seek to make Him king.

But Jesus would have no part in being made King or in challenging the Romans. He encouraged His followers to "render unto Caesar those things that are Caesar's and unto God those things that are God's." He allowed a tax gatherer, a social pariah, to be His disciple suggesting that He didn't believe in 'guilt by association' nor was He interested in winning the approval of the masses. He walked away from crowds that desired to make Him King. As to violence, He preached that "those who live by the sword die by the sword." In his last days, He came into Jerusalem riding on a donkey to underscore His approach was peaceful, without risk to the powers that be. Still, the implied threat remained – due to His popularity with the common people and His public display of malice toward the religious leadership – both factors setting Him on the pathway to crucifixion. With religious and civil powers fixed in place, their selfish agendas settled, and the momentum of events increasing, His death was inevitable.

Religion burns hot in tumultuous times. It's no different today. With one crisis building upon the next, there's no respite for the anxious. Unsolvable problems mount. Matters are made worse as time goes forward. We can't seem to quiet this tumult. Cable news incessantly broadcasts the latest developments, 7 by 24. As I write these words, Japan faces a nuclear meltdown brought on by a 9.0 earthquake while seeking to overcome the effects of a killer Tsunami. At least 20,000 Japanese are feared dead. On the other side of the world, Islamic social unrest and wars in the Middle East consume no less than six separate nations, highlighted by the attack of Western coalition armies on Libya's military and dictator, Muammar Gadhafi. Happily, the Israeli-Palestinian conflict is temporarily hushed as these other stories occupy the headlines. However, we know this situation will not remain quiet for long. Iran continues aggressive action to create a nuclear weapon threatening to throw the entire region into war. Domestically, prices for food and for energy continue to rise. Unemployment increases and governments sit on the brink of bankruptcy. People everywhere are beginning to panic, assuming the next mega disaster will occur on *their doorstep.*

Lest we think our problems are only temporary, intellectual 'think tanks' remind us that food shortages are with us to stay. The rising cost of energy reduces the chance for economic recovery; even advances in medicine, information technology, communication, and agriculture all could back-fire as we introduce dramatic new technologies producing unintended consequences. Future climate scenarios forecast stronger hurricanes, more extremes in temperature, and coastal flooding as ice packs in the Arctic and Antarctic relentlessly melt away. It's obvious we are not masters of nature.

In the U.S., prospects for improving our lot diminish as we move toward tomorrow. Most Americans opine the so-called *American Dream* is dead. We anticipate our children's lives will enjoy much less prosperity than what we've experienced – a gloomy expectation indeed never present before in American economic forecasts.

Over the past two decades, our popular culture grows increasingly edgy. Movies, television shows, and documentaries play on our fears, presenting catastrophes as entertainment. Disaster movies, frequently starring frightful aliens from outer space, are standard fare. Since entertainment is an escape from everyday difficulties, our captivation is all the more surprising given these 'getaways' reinforce our helplessness against overwhelming forces always beyond our control.

We seek other kinds of relief in the strangest places with the worst substances we can manufacture. Our society has never been more addicted to hard alcohol, recreational drugs, overeating, consumerism, and sex. If we aren't eating ourselves to death, we forfeit our future, purchasing ourselves into such deep debt our only relief comes through extraordinary measures. What's worse, our favorite pastime is staring enthralled at Hollywood celebrities doubling as icons for our moral breakdown. Their addictions and bad behavior feed our insatiable appetite for scandal.

What can satisfy the hunger of our souls? Popular religions spin cosmologies more outlandish and over the top than ever. Pseudo-spiritual movements hype their mystical solutions for these tempestuous times. The 2012 phenomenon has generated scads of books and self-help DVDs during this first part of the 21st century. Study shows, however, the core issue for those captivated by 2012 is not the end of the world, but the crisis of personal and political choice. In many ways, this 'movement' is nothing more than a relabeled New Age pseudo-religion which dominated spiritual discussions during the last third of the 20th century. In the final analysis, those that are *tuned into* this new spirituality are *turned on* to drugs, yoga, meditation, and spiritual disciplines whose practice promises *psychic reality* – a titillating 'high' absent in religious experience of common folk. Even more telling, the acceptance of the supernatural is astounding. Movies and television shows based on the paranormal are legion. The History Channel, that bastion of well-documented truths, celebrates belief in extraterrestrials as nurturing parents to the human race. UFO documentaries are replete with undeniable encounters of the unknown. How the scene has changed from the secularism and skepticism of the 1960's and 70's! Once upon a time, we strained to believe anything 'out of the ordinary' – now, we accept whatever's whacky and 'out of this world' in due course.

Underlying all of these gimmicks to find meaning lurks a 'creeping death' – a deep despair regarding Western civilization rooted in our dissatisfaction with the 'old ways of thinking.' Decades ago (centuries ago in Europe), we advocated principles originating in the Bible. We accepted a transcendent basis for law that guaranteed absolute truth. Practicing ethics in business mattered to most of us because we didn't separate our spirituality from secular pursuits. Since we accepted the notion of an all-seeing, all-knowing God whose laws demanded justice and compassion, we expended considerable time and effort in charitable activities.

Similarly, not that long ago in America, accountability wasn't consciously evaded but implicitly embraced. Taking responsibility personally or corporately to 'make things right' or 'do the right thing' was standard operating procedure. But today, we calculate the downside: "Why worry about it? To whom do we answer? If we can cheat and get away with it, why wouldn't we?" Ethics is a forgotten word and a lost art.

Nowadays, we much prefer to think of God as a reality 'residing within.' Harkening to ages old 'metaphysics' plagiarized from eastern mysticism then mixed with 'modern' physics, we've chopped God down to size. The notion of God only serves as a subtle encouragement to be 'centered' and thoughtful – but primarily directed at the person we care about most – *me*. We've adopted a pantheistic piety. Today, it's all about us. Consequently, when we choose to acknowledge the divine, we can now place His (his) name in lower case. What's more, since we perceive our deepest problems result from our failure to be *in touch with ourselves*, only we need take responsibility for our reclamation. Apparently, by accepting our personal divinity, we gain power to live, love, and be happy.

However, some gurus and spiritual guides advocate a much more radical departure from our Western religious past. They promise new answers to satisfy our personal needs and rectify our political problems once we cast away the archaic notions of the *old order* – guidelines that are inflexible, materialistic, and legalistic. In some cases (such as in the movement self-named "Awakening as One"), subtle threats lie buried within its message of 'hope' challenging all inquirers to change to this new way of thinking or face the devastating consequences! Those who do not fall in line – who do not choose 'to sing out of the same hymnbook' with these spiritualists – won't make the transition to the 'new age' (an epoch they predict arrives on or soon after the end of 2012 of course). The 'non-illuminated' will be eliminated. What's the means to exterminate the uncommitted? The next inquisition's tools aren't plainly disclosed as of yet. But since the philosophy behind this program was rooted in Nazism (to be specific, esoteric

Theosophy), we should worry whether a second holocaust hides in the plans of its activists.*

When we turn to social and political matters, do we find hope there? Are the old ways, those principles upon which America was founded, truly outdated? Is the dismissal of God from our government (virtually a *fait accompli* at this moment), likely to benefit our populace from whom the consent to be governed is derived? As a nation, do we still desire, "In God We Trust" printed on our currency?

Assume for a moment that Jesus Christ was invited to speak to a joint session of the United States Congress. Would He praise our government for the way it's managing things? Or would Jesus challenge our nation's leaders to see the signs indicating America's future is ever-so fragile? Would He praise us for our democratic ideals or rebuke us for our failure to live up to the principles our political philosophy advocates? Would He champion the American cause or criticize us for turning America's 'exceptionalism' into an idol justifying whatever course of action we take on the world scene? Would He predict good times ahead or proclaim how blind we are to the consequences of our chosen paths?

One thing's for sure: Jesus had no tolerance for hypocrites. If we act out of self-interest He would distinctly warn us, "Don't insist your motivation is solely for 'the expansion of democracy!' For when you promote or sustain dictators in the world only because they protect American interests, it's best you make no claim to morality as your motive. To do otherwise is not only disingenuous, it is deceitful and detrimental. You fool and harm no one except yourselves!"

---

* I discuss this possibility in more depth in my book, *Decoding Doomsday*, in the chapter on esotericism, UFOs, and Nazism. This is also the conclusion of the authors of *The Stargate Conspiracy,* Lynn Picknett and Clive Prince.

At the very least, Jesus would insist we face the facts. He didn't mince words in His day and He wouldn't now. He would advise: "Speak truthfully and act accordingly. Too many political decisions arise from the selfish agendas of your leaders who primarily seek to maintain their power and position rather than ensure what they achieve serves the best interests of their constituents – and not just the special interest groups or the wealthy who court their favor with campaign donations and boondoggles."

And yet, it's not just the leadership that's to blame. The populace spends too much time caught up in 'life as usual' – soaking up entertainment rather than taking stock of what's wrong with society and *how we can correct it*. No doubt a related but distinct challenge we face (if we are to alter our course) resides in the ineffectiveness of our political and social systems themselves. The bureaucracy looms everywhere; like a castle with unassailable walls, any thought of attack overwhelms us. Our 'canons' of good intent are no match. No matter how hard the cannonball may strike, the castle walls are unrelenting.

What's worse, we are a nation divided. We debate almost every substantive issue with the outcome predetermined based on 'party lines' (i.e., which party holds the majority). This 'double-mindedness' in America stokes the fire of internal contempt, paralyzing us from attaining change. Perhaps the only fix for what's wrong with our political and social structures is for a 'vocal majority' to emerge which enables real transformation to occur; for only broad agreement can foster dramatic moves. But what kind of concurrence would be necessary? Where must we find common ground?

Unless dramatic modification in the viewpoints of a super majority occurs within our nation regarding (1) the moral fabric comprising who we are individually, (2) what values we extol culturally, and (3) what ideals drive our goals politically, we won't garner sufficient leverage to change course.

What's worse, *the fuel foot pedal in our 'vehicle' (i.e., our nation and its ways of doing things) remains fully depressed.* We travel at maximum speed. All this transpires while we approach a cliff set in our path by years of economic mismanagement. How can we adjust the direction we're heading with such an overblown bureaucracy spending more money feeding itself than administering services to others? Aren't we like a railroad locked onto its tracks? How can we slow the momentum caused by so many poor choices and the escalating but often unforeseen challenges which arise daily?

Just like the nation of Israel in the first century, we stand perched on the precipice of national ruination. If we can't steer a different course and unstick the accelerator, we will soon plunge headlong into the abyss of international mediocrity and domestic turmoil inevitably resulting in 'injustice for many.' Our fate could be similar to Israel in the first century AD. God established Israel to be a 'light unto the gentiles.' Instead, it was no longer a light even unto itself. Is that not true about America today? Are we any different than ancient Israel? If the Messiah appeared in this moment calling us to national repentance, wouldn't His fate be similar to Jesus of Nazareth in the first century? Is there any hope that America stands ready to make life-changing choices personally, culturally, and politically? Does America have the will to chart a different course?

No doubt we can build an impressive case asserting 'nothing happens in the world for good' unless America leads the way. We can boast we are now the only superpower on the planet. Both of these statements are true. I admit I share in American pride and what this implies about our great nation. But *from those whom much is expected, much is required.* For on the other hand, it's simple to make a counter-argument: America allows itself to be drawn into many of its policies and actions by the choices of other nations and powerful figures outside the United States. To press this further: America's affirmation of self-determination and sovereignty has become more than mere delusion; it verges on suicidal self-deception.

This negative assessment stems from the obvious intention of the 'globalists' to eradicate nationalistic sentiments worldwide. The specter of international government manifests itself more and more fully, year after year. America's strength continues to thwart its realization even while American leadership is a mainstay toward the achievement of this elitist plan to gain world-wide control. Ostensibly, this quiet revolution foisted upon us by 'the Captains and the Kings'[†] is dedicated to making things better for everyone on the planet. But intrinsically, it's about the rich preserving their wealth and privileged position. This clandestine plan, the conspiracy of the super-wealthy organized through both secretive and not-so-secretive groups, represents 'the shadow government' whose behind the scenes domination pretends the betterment of all the world's people. But can an elite motivated by 'reason only' solve our problems?[‡] Certainly, the sheep dare not speak against these unelected shepherds, lest we be accused of paranoia or intransigence. Since most don't take such a conspiracy seriously and those that do remain mostly silent, nationally we sit poised to relinquish to these wealthy 'few' what meager authority America retains in hopes these elites will build a better world.

So is the apocalypse near? From many perspectives, it certainly appears inevitable. But whether it commences soon,

---

[†] A book by this title, authored by Taylor Caldwell, was made into mini-series in 1976. It was loosely based on the Kennedy's and presented a case that financiers and the politicians they own are the real protagonists on the world stage. Democracy is illusory.
[‡] This is the stated goal of Freemasonry, Rosicrucianism, and other secret societies seeking world domination, however righteous they purpose their influence to be. The writings of Albert Pike and Manly Hall, 33° Freemasons, and intellectual founders of the 'Craft' as Freemasonry refers to it, make this goal plain.

• • •

several decades from now, or beyond – more than ever before – I profess the only hope for our troubled nation and our world *is the truth of the Bible and its prescriptions for our personal lives, our culture, and our nation.* Many will object to this assertion; the tag-line likely being, 'been there, done that.' However, 'wherever we were and whatever we did' failed to resemble what true Christianity teaches and true spirituality demands. Those meant to serve as 'salt' in the world lost their savor.

In the last 100 years, America's pulpits have been compromised by clergy whose vitality for Christianity was drained by the intellectual bankruptcy of naturalism (through its denial of the miraculous) and the attempt to accommodate the Christian gospel to an unbiblical form of truth. As Francis Schaeffer, a noted Christian intellectual assessed, modern theology split truth between two spheres: (1) 'Spiritual' matters and (2) scientific or historical 'factual' matters. By agreeing with this definition of 'truth' encouraged by the conclusions of what is known in theology as 'higher criticism' (purporting the gospel is contaminated by folklore, myth, and unscientific presuppositions of ancient times), Christian 'truth' became detached from rationality (and reality).§ This 'escape from reason' led to a terminal case of anemia for the mainline Protestant Christian Church and in many cases, Catholicism as well. Christianity lost its voice as it lost touch with its historic understanding of the nature and reality of God.

The Christian message isn't relevant to most members of our society not because it was tried and found wanting; but because many of its teachers today and in the recent past rarely

---

§ Religious truth became a sense of moral obligation (Kant); a 'feeling of absolute dependence' (Schleiermacher); a mere projection of the human mind (Feuerbach); mystical encounters (James); an 'ultimate experience' (Tillich and Jasper); semantic mysticism (Ogden); or simply justification for political action (Liberation theology).

• • •

represented the most essential elements of the gospel of Christ, leading too few converts to commit themselves to its fulfillment. Modernist 'priests' ceased preaching an authentic gospel when they jettisoned elements *fundamental* to the gospel, in particular the biblical catchphrase *"The Kingdom of God is coming!"* Fearing the accusation of preaching 'hell, fire, and brimstone' too few ministers heralded what Jesus proclaimed, "Repent and believe – before it's too late!" It's crucial for it is this element which catalyzes all other aspects of Christ's solution for humankind. When the gospel of Christ doesn't include a strong dose of apocalyptic fervor, the audience interprets the offer of salvation as a 'take it or leave it' proposition. *True Christianity* and *true spirituality* (what we believe and how we put it into practice) are founded on the premise *our time in this life is short* – every moment counts. And yet, in the short period we have on this planet, we leave a legacy – good or bad. Each and every day our actions leave an indelible imprint in the fabric of time. Our lives either enhance the weave in the tapestry or disfigure its picture. We choose the impression we wish to leave.

Does the Bible have answers for today? Of course. If we adopted biblical truth (willingly and widely to guide us personally, culturally, and politically), the result would change the world. However, I fear our society has passed the point of no return. While the gospel of Jesus Christ teaches *how we should live* and *why this lifestyle provides hope and meaning*, I have little optimism that repentance remains an option on the table. I sincerely hope I'm wrong. Yet, I fear our society has wandered too far away from the path of honesty and virtue to find its way back. Indeed, there's little hope we can agree on a moral code that's pertinent to all; much less a code the majority will follow. A return to 'traditional values' in America simply isn't in the cards. After all, a transition like this would be too politically incorrect. "Everyone should just do what's right in their own eyes. That will cause the least friction" (I say this sarcastically of course!)

Given the inertia for meaningful change, what will we do? We can apply band aids. Bailing wire and paper clicks can be put to use. We can improve the political situation somewhat with a few better decisions and by electing leaders who strive for a more just and equitable society. We can and should relieve suffering whenever we find it. We can find a measure of personal peace and hope in the days ahead. But all these measures, even if taken together, won't yield a permanent fix.

There remains only one foundation from which to build an enduring hope: The culmination of history, specifically our destiny as expressed through the words of the New Testament. Modernists will complain: "At best this is a dereliction of duty! At worst it is a grand delusion!" But that's *the gospel truth*. As we will soon show, it's plainly what Jesus taught. Likewise, His Apostles institutionalized this expectation at the beginning of His church. Even as the first century came to a close and the Lord had not returned, we see throughout the 'patristic period' leading up to St. Augustine, the soon coming of the Lord was strenuously upheld. It was essential to the Church's message.

The dark predictions of what lies ahead – a sun *black* like a sackcloth of hair and a moon turned *blood red* – are merely the most dramatic of many ominous signs depicted in the last days by the Bible. Not long ago, almost everyone agreed these images were no more than imaginative symbols. However, such frightening pictures no longer seem too fantastic to happen in space-time. Many scenarios suggest how such horrible sights could become the standard way our 'sky lights' appear. In this regard, it's easier than ever to be a Bible literalist.

What doubles the impact of evidence for the approaching apocalypse isn't fanciful interpretation of Scripture nor is it a consensus of the world's religions that the end is near. Rather, it's science, a most surprising ally, which forecasts impending, perhaps insurmountable catastrophes. Comet collisions crashing into our planet, unprecedented solar activity destroying our electrical grid, stresses on earth's tectonic plates generating massive earthquakes, unprecedented climate change killing off entire species, and biological threats (be they natural or manmade) which could destroy life altogether. Pick your poison: Potential calamities abound.

Whether we choose to accept what the Bible predicts, or whether we simply acknowledge what science projects concerning the future, either source tells the same story: We seem destined for doomsday. It isn't a question of if, but how soon. Consequently, the pages ahead underscore our confidence and hope comes from (1) a better understanding of what the Bible says is soon coming to pass and (2) what we must do to escape these cataclysms and (3) most notably, the amazing experience to anticipate thereafter.

In both my previous books, I asserted that authentic Christianity *is an apocalyptic religion* – and should rightly continue to be so even to this day. However, I did not put forth in those books anything more than a cursory argument for why a preoccupation with biblical prophecy is pivotal to our preparedness as believers. It's my hope that this gap is addressed by *Black Sun, Blood Moon*. After demonstrating the premise that Christianity is an apocalyptic faith by drawing upon the original biblical texts, I turn my focus to how the promise of Christ's return provides hope – and how that hope makes a difference in our lives today as we face many upheavals in the months and years ahead. Furthermore, I intend to answer the question, "How can we obtain confidence and optimism about the future despite the dismal state of our world and its prospects for substantive change?"

For those who believe in Jesus Christ, we have no excuse if we fail to study Bible prophecy and understand the 'times and seasons.' Our inheritance as the children of God includes His Word in the Bible: We can learn *what happens next* and *what the world to come is like*. If we regard ourselves disciples of Jesus Christ, this should be a priority. Jesus taught His disciples these very truths. Moreover, it ought to be our priority from a practical standpoint: We gain perspective on where we must ground our hope. Once we come to realize the stark contrast between what humanity plans for this world compared to what it means for the Kingdom of God to come into this world, we can reorient our viewpoint finding true purpose, real meaning, and an enduring hope. We will be empowered afresh to display the love of Christ within our relationships, experience peace in these troubled times, and exude courage to face the challenges ahead.

But before you conclude that I'm totally ready to flush the future down the toilet and take no responsibility for what happens in the world 'until Jesus comes back,' let me make a few additional remarks to clarify my position and conclude this introduction.

Believing in the 'second coming' actually increases the impact Christians make upon the world — now. It makes the world a better place. Historically, this has been shown to be true. The first Americans believed they were to be the 'shining city on a hill' paving the way for the millennial reign of the Messiah. When revivals broke out in our country (several times, the so-called *Great Awakenings* of which there were four), many important political advances were achieved.** It may seem

---

** "Joseph Tracy, the minister and historian who gave this religious phenomenon its name in his influential 1842 book *The Great Awakening*, saw the First Great Awakening as a precursor to the American Revolution. The evangelical movement of the 1740s played a key role in the development of democratic concepts in the period of the American Revolution. This helped create a demand for the separation of church and state." (See en.wikipedia.org /wiki/Great Awakening).

ironic. *But believing in the world soon to come enables us to have greater influence on the world we live in today.* It energizes our commitment. Once we become convinced of the coming Kingdom, transformation begins in the 'here and now.'

Within these pages, I share with the reader amazing truths regarding what happens in the years ahead. By knowing what's coming upon the earth, we prepare ourselves to deal with the pending challenges. Likewise, by providing the Bible's perspective on the 'hope for the hereafter,' we gain deep confidence in our ability to withstand the challenges of today. Finally, I applaud and encourage activities that promote peace, social justice, and building stronger relationships among families, groups, diverse cultures, and nations. I say this despite my belief that our most vital hope lies exclusively in a peculiar type of new world order called for by the Judeo-Christian scriptures and our nation's early heritage. Therefore, I champion the original gospel *byword* and the consistent insistence of His followers through the ages: *The Kingdom of God is at hand!* Will we embrace this reality or hide from it? The choice is ours.

* * * * *

One final word of preface: Many authors on spiritual subjects, in particular biblical prophecy, seldom ask their readers to carefully and prayerfully ponder what they've written. Generally, we aren't encouraged to meditate on how we can take biblical truth 'to heart.' However, I estimate the distance between our heads and hearts is further than it appears. We must be encouraged to ruminate on what we read. Jesus said, "He who has ears to hear, let him hear!" This was His way of expressing "May my words soak into your ears!"

In this volume, I hope to *encourage* as well as *educate* the reader. I offer the following 'essays' as extended devotions that may be read many times. Consequently, I've structured them as both studies and meditations: (1) Providing a primary Bible verse up front as a focal point, (2) offering my analysis and commentary, and lastly, (3) posing contemplative questions to help the reader reflect on what's been read, hoping that any and all learning is put to good, practical use.

With that in mind, I might also suggest interested groups read the book together and use the questions at the end of each chapter as a means to stimulate discussion. Because I anticipate that the book will be put to use in this way, I do provide a bit of redundancy repeating the definition of a few key terms in several of the chapters. I beg the reader's forgiveness for this design element. Knowing that group members will miss a week or two, I don't assume every reader will read the chapters in sequence and may not read all the right chapters before jumping into the discussion! Please bear with this slight distraction.

In conclusion, I feel confident that many good results can be encouraged by this work. I offer it to you, the reader, in that hopeful spirit.

1: Christianity – An Apocalyptic Faith

Watch ye therefore: for ye know not when the master of the house
cometh, at even, or at midnight, or at the cockcrowing,
or in the morning (Mark 13:35)

Watch therefore, for ye know neither the day nor the hour
wherein the Son of man cometh. (Matthew 25:13)

JESUS CHRIST WAS THE WORLD'S GREATEST TEACHER. WHAT MADE HIM SO EFFECTIVE WAS HIS CLEVER USE OF ILLUSTRATIONS FAMILIAR TO COMMON PEOPLE. His most popular teaching method was the parable. Through His parables, Jesus employed many vivid but quaint images. In one of his 50 plus parables, he tell us a story of a woman who lost a coin of great value and had to sweep her house carefully to find it. Once uncovered, she called all of her neighbors together to share in her joy. In another parable, Jesus compared the Kingdom of God to an expensive pearl. The Kingdom was like a 'pearl of great price,' so desired by one particular man, he sold everything he owned to purchase it.

Jesus compared God to a judge in some parables or to a master of a vineyard in others; both told stories explaining what God demands of His servants. Some of these stories were allegories – tales whose characters represented people in real life. One in particular portrayed 'workers in the vineyard' whose master requested they guard the vineyard while he traveled overseas. Several times the master sent his closest stewards to check up on things. However, in each case the workers killed the servant the master sent. Eventually, the master sent his son, assuming that they would pay attention to him. Instead, the workers elected to kill the son too, thinking by so doing they would inherit the vineyard! Not only does this story illustrate Jesus knew beforehand He would soon be put to death, but also that it would be the religious leaders (who worked in His 'vineyard') that would commit this improbable act. The 'workers of the vineyard' proved to be the master's mortal enemies.

Jesus employed another simple tool: The comparison between earthly facts and spiritual truths. For instance, salt was a powerful commodity in His day. Salt not only enhanced the flavor of food, salt preserved it. In the days long before refrigerators, salt was a miracle compound. Jesus educated His followers to be like salt: "Take responsibility, enhance the world around you, and act as a preservative." If His followers didn't 'salt' people and circumstances, the world would suffer.

Jesus engaged the simile of *light* in another comparison. His believers were to be *as light*. To maximize their brightness, they shouldn't be placed on the floor. Rather they should be placed on a stand, elevated, to enlighten everyone in the room. We could say Jesus set high expectations for His disciples!

In these plain teachings, Jesus insisted His followers be responsible for preserving and transforming the world in which they live. If they don't perform this service, they're worthless and ought to be thrown into the rubbish heap. And yet, Jesus introduced these admonitions in the context of dramatic changes. Jesus warned of *judgment* (*krisis*, in the Greek from which our word *crisis* is derived). Like John before Him, Jesus proclaimed a radical and imminent alteration to society.

The teaching of Jesus Christ and His Apostles in the New Testament calls for conversion and repentance. Yet, it remains grounded firmly in the conviction that humankind left to its own devices will never achieve a perfect society. Individuals without a spiritual rebirth can never know God. Transforming persons and (perhaps in some cases) human institutions, may demand intervention by God in the space-time world. These 'involvements' may be invisible – like the Holy Spirit (*pneuma* in Greek, aka *the wind* or more precisely, the *breath of God*) – who blows where He wills while remaining invisible. Yet, we see the Spirit's effects. (See John Chapter 3).

God's actions intersect the human domain. Whether visible or not, when God touches history in this way, like a river, the waters drastically change course. The incarnation is God's ultimate *intrusion*. Jesus' presence set this *new course*. The river now flows through different banks and on an alternate riverbed. Jesus' agenda was to radically alter the world. His tagline was the announcement of a new Kingdom. "Behold, the Kingdom of God is here." The message itself is an *apocalypse* – an unveiling, which is what the term *apocalypse* means. That's why the final book of the Bible is called both "The Revelation of Jesus Christ" and "The Apocalypse of Jesus Christ." The terms are interchangeable. In this sense, the arrival of Jesus Christ on the world scene and the 33 years He spent on this earth was *the first apocalypse* – the first unveiling. His incarnation revealed what God is truly like. The return of this same Christ at His *Second Coming* is the "second apocalypse." At this next revealing, we will discover much more concerning the nature of God. Upon this recognition, we discover the very 'heart and soul' of the Christian faith is *apocalypse* – it's the revelation of God to His people.

Hence, since Christianity is 'apocalyptic' at its core, the following thesis seems appropriate to place here at the outset:

Any Christianity which denies the Second Coming of Jesus Christ to this earth as a 'space-time' reality is inconsistent with the spoken words of Jesus of Nazareth as proclaimed in the four canonical gospels.

There are various arguments, indeed whole schools of thought, concerning exactly *when* Jesus will return and under what circumstances. These are important matters; but none more important than the question of whether or not He will *physically* return. This reappearance is scheduled at the culmination of history. Consequently, any 'gospel'* that obscures the apocalyptic message of Jesus Christ and His disciples has no sincere claim to continuity with New Testament teaching. The essence of this argument builds upon numerous and plainly stated biblical themes. I cite five of them as follows.

First, the vital announcement of Jesus Christ was, *"The time is fulfilled. The Kingdom of God is at hand! Repent ye and believe in the gospel"* (See Mark 1: 15). During the past two centuries, theologians turned this proclamation into symbolic mishmash. That might be fine if Jesus didn't mention Hebrew Scripture to authenticate His ministry. But he did so repeatedly. Jesus knew why He was here. He clearly regarded Himself as the fulfillment of the messianic prophecies in the Old Testament. After John the Baptist had been imprisoned and was somewhat demoralized, John asked his disciples to inquire of Jesus if He was the 'anointed one' or should the Jews be looking for some other. The account in Luke records the unmistakable answer – Jesus quoting messianic predictions in the book of Isaiah:

> *And John calling unto him two of his disciples sent them to Jesus, saying, "Art thou he that should come or look we for another?" When the men were come unto him, they said, "John [the] Baptist hath sent us unto thee, saying, "Art thou he that should come or look we for another?" And in that same hour He cured many of their infirmities and plagues, and of evil spirits; and unto many that were blind He gave sight. Then Jesus answering said unto them, "Go your way, and tell John what things ye have seen and heard; how that the blind see, the lame walk, the lepers are cleansed, the deaf hear, the dead are raised, to the poor the gospel is preached. And blessed is he, whosoever shall not be offended in Me" (Luke 7:19-21).*

---

* *Gospel* in the Greek is *evangelion*, meaning *'good tidings'* or *'good news.'*

Scores of other passages could be quoted demonstrating that Jesus was crystal clear about His purpose. While the phrase *Kingdom of God* is present in 69 New Testament verses, the earliest gospel, the *Gospel of Mark*, expresses the exact phrase 15 times. Jews understood the Kingdom in the Hebrew context of the *Davidic* Kingdom. While the 'dying Messiah' contradicted the Jewish hope for a conquering Christ, Christianity insists it's through His vicarious sufferings and death the righteous 'enter into this Kingdom.' Christians believe the Hebrew Scriptures plainly describe both aspects of the Messiah.[†] But it's no surprise that the oppressed Jews of Jesus' day much preferred the *Conquering Christ* to the *Suffering Servant*. The Hebrews had been suffering too long already!

Nevertheless, repentance must come first. John's ministry of baptism signaled the priority of cleansing oneself of sin before one can enter into the Kingdom. Jesus sought the repentance of the Hebrew nation, principally as reflected in the acceptance (or rejection) of its leadership. However, it became clear from the very beginning of His ministry, Jesus of Nazareth would not change the 'hearts and minds' of the ruling class. Like most political and religious leaders today, the Pharisees, Sadducees, and royal house of the Herodians had no interest in changing the status quo. While they unanimously hated the occupying Roman force, when it came time to deal with Jesus – whose message represented a radical modification for their civil society and religious practice – they set aside their differences and banded together. Leveraging their authority and armed guards, they executed Jesus, suppressed His followers, and maintained the existing order. Surely, the Kingdom of Man was not ready for the Kingdom of God.

[†] Read Chapter 53 of Isaiah and Psalm 22 to see this suffering Christ expressed in the Old Testament.

Of course, thousands of the common folk and a few of the occupying Roman force embraced Jesus' message. We remember the words of a particular Roman centurion who had built a synagogue for the Jewish village under his care, asking Jesus just to say the word and his servant would be healed. (See Matthew 8:5-13) Jesus was astonished. He remarked that this Roman understood the essence of faith better than any Hebrew in the entire country.[‡] The gospel writer tells us as a result of such great faith, Jesus healed the centurion's servant at the very moment He 'issued the order' for the servant to be made well. There was no delay.

The second factor demanding we accept the literal Second Advent of Jesus Christ stems from the Savior's dispatch to Heaven. At the beginning of the *Book of Acts* we read the dramatic account of His ascension. A cloud approached and took him away. Then angels appeared, asking His disciples (paraphrasing), "Why are you all standing around, looking up into the sky? This same Jesus will descend, just as you have seen him ascend. It will be in the very same manner." (See Acts, Chapter 1) What did the angels mean? Simply this: "Get busy; there's no time to waste. Stop being awed by what you have just seen – remarkable though it may be. Your mission launches now!" From the very beginning, the growth of the Church of Jesus Christ was predicated upon the imminent return of their Savior. His next advent could not have been more foundational.

However, the disciples remembered Jesus' instruction to wait for the coming of the Holy Spirit before kicking off their

---

[‡] The key to the Centurion's faith was his understanding the linkage between faith and authority; more specifically, that Jesus had authority over spirits, sickness, and all the forces repressing humankind. With a single command, Jesus made the servant well.

efforts. *"And, behold, I send the promise of my Father upon you: but tarry ye in the city of Jerusalem, until ye be endued with power from on high" (Luke 24:49).* To be effective in their mission, they needed a power boost! We should also make careful note that while this descent of the Spirit of Christ was a 'second coming' of sorts, it wasn't *in the same manner.* The disciples weren't confused on this matter. Peter, their leader, indicated the miraculous signs witnessed in the streets of Jerusalem (the 'unlearned' speaking in tongues they did not know – *real languages*, not gibberish – telling of the wonderful acts of God), revealed to his audience that they lived *in the last days* just as the prophet Joel had predicted (Acts 2:6-18, Joel 2:28). Having receiving the Spirit of Christ, Peter preached the need for repentance, particularly since the Son of God had been crucified by the country's leadership (Acts 2:22, 23). The Messiah, the one for whom they had been waiting for over 1,000 years, was dead as a result of their actions. Peter pushed his finger directly into the wound. This was an issue of national shame. The crowd reacted with horror. What should they do? "Repent" he said, "And be baptized for the remission of your sins and ye shall receive the Holy Ghost [Spirit]" (Acts 2:38). Jesus' death was all part of God's preordained plan just as Peter had conveyed. However, he explained this same Messiah would return again – the next time bringing the Kingdom in full force. As a result of his inspired preaching, 3,000 persons were added to their number.

In addition to the evangelistic directive of Jesus to his disciples, *"Go ye therefore and teach all nations,"* (Matthew 28:19) which as history records resulted in "the world turned upside down,"[§] the gospels weave a prediction throughout

---

§ Another key point being that it was the anticipation of a soon return which drove the disciples forward with such fervor. Believing in

their accounts (and later in the epistles of the Apostles): History will culminate in a time of *great tribulation*. There will be distressing realities of earthquakes, plagues, famine, and portents so awesome that *"men's hearts [will] fail them for fear"* of what is soon to come upon the earth (Luke 21:26). This is the third major reason for acknowledging the importance of the Second Advent of Jesus Christ: The Apostles warn us *we must prepare for the coming cataclysms.* Soon God will judge humankind for their wickedness.

But importantly, in this context, Jesus makes a remarkable commitment to His followers: *"Watch ye therefore, and pray always, that ye may be accounted worthy to escape all these things that shall come to pass, and to stand before the Son of Man"* (Luke 21:36). Jesus tells of a way to escape from these horrors. While there is great debate about the exact timing of His coming for *"those found worthy,"*** His promise remains; before the worst happens, Jesus 'catches up' His followers and escorts them to heaven. Paul clarifies this matter of how Jesus returns for His followers: *"Then we which are alive (and) remain shall be **caught up** (harpazo in the Greek and rapturae in Latin) together with them (the dead) in the clouds, to meet the Lord in the air: And so shall we ever be with the Lord"* (I Thessalonians 4:17). The gospel of Christ and its salvation proclaims *deliverance from the wrath of God to come* (I Thessalonians 1:10, Romans 5:9).

Many know this event – the Rapture – as *"the blessed hope of the Church"* (See Titus 2:13). Even for those who deny that this

---

the Second Coming as an imminent event implies "Time is short. We best get the word out to everyone as quickly as we can." This mind-set inspired and energized the actions of the early church.
** To be found worthy, we are required to "receive Him" (John 1:12). We are saved by His grace through our faith, a gift of God, not as a result of anything we have done (Romans 3:24).

amazing event could happen at any moment (but steadfastly believe Christ will return to this earth), the Rapture remains a sacred promise of Jesus. Christ's coming for His church stands unquestionably as a major component of His teaching and of all His apostles. †† There is little dispute to this fact. *"Therefore you do not lack any spiritual gift as you eagerly wait for our Lord Jesus Christ to be revealed. He will also keep you firm to the end, so that you will be blameless on the day of our Lord Jesus Christ"* (I Corinthians 1:7, 8; I John 4:17, New International Version).

But what does Christ command His followers to do in the meantime? This is the issue of "until." This comprises the fourth key reason to believe in His imminent return: Jesus commands us "to watch." *Being watchful is not optional.* Many times in His teaching, Jesus warned His followers to remain alert:

- **Watch** *ye therefore: for ye know not when the master of the house cometh, at even, or at midnight, or at the cock-crowing, or in the morning* (Mark 13:35)

- **Watch** *therefore: for ye know not what hour your Lord doth come* (Matthew 24:42)

- **Watch** *therefore, for ye know neither the day nor the hour wherein the Son of man cometh.* (Matthew 25:13)

As Jesus taught, when the watchful see, *"these things begin to come to pass, then [they will] look up for [their] redemption draweth nigh."* (Luke 21:28) For those who are *"children of the day"* (according to Paul) ought not to be surprised by

---

†† Many committed believers in Christ believe the Rapture happens immediately before Jesus physically comes back to the earth, specifically at the Battle of Armageddon. Most believers today, however, believe His return is some period before, from a few months to a few years. Indeed, the most common view is at least seven years before.

what happens. They should *recognize the signs of His soon coming* (I Thessalonians 5:5). It's this same missive Paul delivered to his churches. He instructs his disciples not to falter in upholding its truthfulness: *"Whereunto he called you by our gospel, to the obtaining of the glory of our Lord Jesus Christ. Therefore, brethren, stand fast, and* **hold the traditions** *which ye have been taught, whether by word, or our epistle."* (II Thessalonians 2:14, 15).

Finally (and fifthly!), Christ's return completes *a vital aspect of the salvation Christians will enjoy*. Salvation commences with the resurrection from the dead, but concludes with the *glorification of the body* in the very same manner and form as the body of the ascended Christ:

- *Beloved, now are we the sons of God, and it doth not yet appear what we shall be: but we know that, when He shall appear, we shall be like Him; for we shall see Him as He is (I John 3:2)*

- *For whom He did foreknow, He also did predestinate [to be] conformed to the image of His Son, that He might be the firstborn among many brethren (Romans 8:29)*

- *Whereunto he called you by our gospel, to the obtaining of the glory of our Lord Jesus Christ. (II Thessalonians 2:14)*

Until the bodies of those who believe are made like His, their experience of salvation is but a sampling. Much more exists to discover and experience. Christ's gospel promises this.

When we explore the many lessons inherent in the New Testament – that is, those doctrines which comprise its teaching - it becomes apparent how most of its promises are staked upon the coming Kingdom to achieve their final fulfillment. Today, as Paul says, *"We see as in a mirror darkly, but then face-to-face"* (I Corinthians 13:12). What we observe are mere shadows of what is to come. Moreover, should we finally see things as they actually are (in the world to come),

Christians will learn what our former, 'clandestine' mission meant. By shining as 'lights in the world' and 'salting the circumstances' they sought *to embody the vision of this new world coming* – the Kingdom promised by Jesus Christ – who guaranteed its achievement "in the fullness of time" (Ephesians 1:10; Galatians 4: 4).

Today, we watch God's stopwatch ticking toward its apex. Time has all but run its course. The second apocalypse approaches, to use Bob Dylan's words, like "A slow train comin'." How does its proximity alter the path we choose?

FOR FURTHER THOUGHT: Does the idea of the Kingdom of God as the centerpiece of Jesus' teaching seem odd to you? Why was the incarnation necessary? Does it make sense to think in terms of the incarnation as the first Apocalypse? Does the Kingdom of God necessarily entail the coming Apocalypse? What does it mean to 'watch?' as Jesus commanded His disciples? How can we watch for the world to come and still influence the world in which we live today? Do you agree with the statement that our actions today are intended to provide a vision of the 'New World' promised by Jesus Christ? Are you involved in any activity today that compromises your mission? Are you committed to any activity that helps to proclaim the coming Kingdom of God?

2: The Quest to Decipher the Future

*[It is] the glory of God to conceal a thing: but the honor of kings
[is] to search out a matter. (Proverbs 25:2)*

*Remember the former things of old: for I am God, and there is none
else; I am God, and there is none like me, declaring the end from the
beginning, and from ancient times the things that are not yet done,
saying, My counsel shall stand, and I will do all my pleasure
(Isaiah 46:9, 10)*

PERHAPS NO SUBJECT CAPTURES THE ATTENTION OF THE MASSES MORE THAN THE POSSIBILITY WE CAN KNOW WHAT LIES IN THE FUTURE. IN MY LAST BOOK *DECODING Doomsday*, I summarized the many theories regarding what the future holds. I also demonstrated how underlying many efforts of various 'movements' in today's world, lies an attempt to substantiate a pagan, world religion as old as *Sumeria*.* Religions and their prophetic assertions are connected

History demonstrates time-after-time that humankind covets *the truth about the end of the world.* At stake is more than merely discerning how soon the end may be. It's more than just *curiosity* which drives this obsession. It's about *certainty.* For many, the study of prophecy is *the means to determine what worldview is correct.* In other words, prophecy has the power to disclose which religious perspective is right and which others are wrong. Prophecy is a litmus test for what we should believe. As such, we don't just hunger to know the future. We also seek proof that what we believe isn't ludicrous – but truth we can count on. Built into our DNA is the quest for spiritual truth, meaning, *and* certitude. Faith involves all three.

---

* Supposedly humankind's first recorded civilization appearing in the fourth millennium BC within Mesopotamia.

The History Channel presented a documentary recently on history's most famous 'seers' – parading prognosticators galore before its viewers. It spent a good deal of time on modern day prophets as well as the possibility that *precognition* may be an innate faculty in all humankind. The documentary substantiated how occult practice reached its zenith at the end of the 19th century. The extent of belief in the supernatural was widespread. There were millions of subscribers to dozens of journals on spiritualism. Crystal ball gazing, palmistry, and divination of all kinds were frequent 'parlor tricks' which many believed involved more than simple magic. Mediums, palm readers, fortune tellers, and more serious occult practitioners were to be found throughout Europe, England, and America. In this exposé, *the focus was the individual believer and what the future had in store for that specific person.* And yet, the seriousness of the subject underscored there was more to it than just 'checking out the daily horoscope.'

State-side, American *Transcendentalism* in the first half the 19th century (think Ralph Waldo Emerson, Walt Whitman, and Henry David Thoreau) gave way to *Theosophy* in the 1880's (Henry Steel Olcott and Madame Helena Petrovna Blavatsky). These writers provided a philosophical foundation (and some degree of sophistication) for an otherwise purely occult and fantastic worldview. In the former case mere *intuition* was championed whereas in the latter, *channeling spirits* (who pretentiously commented on history, philosophy, as well as predicted the future), was argued to be a more reliable source of knowledge than pure reason.

As documented in my previous writings, Theosophy demands a careful treatment since its ideology is much more serious than merely 'mind over matter.' At the end of the 19th century, it flowered into a syncretistic religion infecting America but Europe in particular, combining Hindu, Buddhist, and pseudo-science into an amalgamation boasting supernatural 'miracles.'

Theosophy prospered from the 1880's until the late 1940's, when it became better known that the Nazi regime based much of its evil upon Theosophy's extreme doctrines asserting Aryanism, occult practices, and a view of history built upon the lost continent of *Atlantis* (The 'Secret Doctrine'). Despite such remarkable mythical beliefs which included the myths of 'fire and ice,' the 'hollow earth,' and racial origins stemming from seven root races of the Atlanteans (spurring the anti-Semitism of Nazism) much of its 'wisdom' was associated with Egyptian mythology. The stories of Isis, Osiris, and Horus would continue to live on in the practice of Freemasonry (and in the more secretive cults of Rosicrucianism and the practice of Alchemy).

Indeed, Freemasonry is perhaps the world's most universal religion – a religion which claims it's no such thing. However, as I've documented elsewhere, Freemasonry is much more than a charitable fraternity. It's built upon a smartly packaged form of paganism, complete with its particular view of God, and especially hope for the afterlife. It too has its own predictions about the future. Masonic prophecies mirror many of what evangelicals hold to be true: It predicts a future world leader will arise, declare his authority in a future Jewish Temple (which they, like orthodox Jews, wish to see rebuilt), and institute a form of government based upon pure reason AND the wisdom of the ancients.[†] This leader is not just to be a clever human being endowed with the gift or oration, but is in fact, purportedly a divine being intent on ruling humankind. The books of Freemasonry intellectuals, Manly P. Hall and Albert Pike, spell out these plans and predictions

---

[†] This is well-documented by Thomas Horn in his book *Apollyon Rising: 2012*, as well as in my book *Decoding Doomsday*, both published by Defender Books. Manly P. Hall's *Secret Destiny of America, in particular* delivers the smoking gun.

in plain English and are available at the local bookstore. There should be no reason to doubt what the mission of Freemasonry is. It is clearly disclosed.‡ It's no surprise evangelicals suspect this forecasted fuehrer to be none other than the Antichrist.

To take this path a bit further: It's captivating how the impact of magicians of the 19th century led to many aspects of the most scientific of US governmental projects: The 20th century space program. In particular, one fascinating person, Jack Parsons who founded the Jet Propulsion Laboratory (JPL), was personally steeped in black *'magick.'* Parson was the head of the Pasadena chapter of *Ordo Templi Orientis* (OTO), an order begun by Samuel Mather at the turn of the 19th century, alongside the infamous Aleister Crowley. Modeled after Freemasonry (both were 33° Freemasons) the order was based upon what members called the *Thelema Law*: "Do what thou wilt shall be the whole of the law" (i.e., "Do whatever you want is our one law – the only law we accept!") Previously in 1935, Parsons married Helen Northrup (a name those in aeronautics will recognize). Parsons was a genuine genius in rocket science, developing solid rocket fuel which overcame many of the dangers with liquid fuel (all too often causing rocket explosions on the launch pad!) His inventions and designs for 'booster rockets' remain the basis for NASA's rocket propulsion systems today. Few know that one of his founding colleagues was a NAZI (Theodore von Kármán) and another conspicuous gentlemen, L. Ron Hubbard *founder of Scientology,* was a Navy spy sent into JPL to keep an eye on these two. Parson and Crowley were great friends until Crowley died in 1947. Hubbard eventually ran off to Florida with Parson's wife, Helen, after Helen's sister, Sara had an affair

---

‡ While most Freemason spokespeople deny they are conspirators or have any such plan for world domination, they never repudiate the writings of Pike or Hall which are unambiguous in this regard.

with Parsons owing to the sexual magick of Crowley. Parson was mysteriously killed in 1952 in his personal laboratory. While declared a suicide, many consider his death murder. L. Ron Hubbard went on to author notable science fiction works and create the Scientology *cosmology* (to many, another form of science fiction), that several public figures in America continue to support (Tom Cruise and John Travolta being the two most famous).

Today, popular attention is focused on 2012 and the possibility that the Mayan Calendar (which culminates on December 21, 2012), signifies the end of humanity. In reality, there is much more to the whole '2012 thing' that just a few predictions that the world is coming to an end. Most of the 'hubbub' about 2012 is actually a loosely formed religion founded on Theosophist roots taking New Age affirmations to the next level. Many of the 2012 books promulgate the transformation of humanity which supposedly culminates late in 2012 (or soon thereafter). This revolution in consciousness links to an old world view that human history is comprised of various 'ages' typically characterized as iron, silver, gold, and finally an age usually sporting a disparaging label, normally associated with the world in which we now live.[§] For instance, the Hindu 'Kali Yuga' is the current age of depravity soon concluding (in 2012 or in about 200 years, the timing depends upon which guru you subscribe to) and yielding the next golden age. Likewise, 'The Age of Aquarius' – for those into astrology – comprises the next age characterized by *enlightenment*. According to the '2012 religion,' true enlightenment requires acquiring a 'higher consciousness' – wherein *we remain in constant contact with the supernatural beings surrounding us* – as well as the inner mindfulness that *we are gods*, capable of infinite possibilities.

[§] The Maya and Aztecs labeled the various epochs 'suns' as do today's Hopi Indians. Ominously, we live at the end of the fifth of five suns.

So it is that the 2012 'movement' is today's most *chic* form of prophecy. In 2012 the transition event – a time of choice – reveals the moment of redemption for humankind or becomes the final straw spelling our doom. If we don't choose wisely, we shall succumb to our atavistic, materialistic, and especially capitalistic behaviors thereby sliding down the slippery slope to ruin. One thing is certain: 2012 thinking isn't likely to find its way into the Republican platform in 2012.

When it comes to prophecy in the historic major religions, we see a distinct increase in the caliber of what is prophesied. Predictions span centuries if not millenniums. Specific prophecies typically involve nations if not the entire globe. And yet, compared to the Judeo-Christian faith, there is relative little emphasis on prophecy. Furthermore, there is little regard for resting the validity of the religion upon its accurate fulfillment. But in the Bible, prophecy matters 'really matter.'

In the case of Evangelicalism, conservative scholars affirm that the authenticity of our faith rests on the spectacular accuracy of what is prophesied in the Bible. In particular, Christianity asserts that Jesus Christ fulfilled scores of prophesies from the Old Testament regarding the nature of the Messiah, His origins, purpose, and destiny. The pinnacle of this 'messianic prophecy' is seen in two particular places spanning entire chapters in the Bible (See Isaiah 53 and Psalm 22). Some say Jesus fulfilled over 60 specific prophecies related to the Messiah.

Whether we profess faith in Jesus as Christ or not, except for the few who are hard-core naturalists (believing humans are purely the product of materialistic evolution), *the vast majority of humankind strives to know why we are here.* We attempt to break the doomsday code because we believe someone smart is (or was) out there, who knows (or knew) about end times and is trying to help us to prepare ourselves for it – or to find a means to avoid it altogether. If we find the most reliable source on predicting the future, we likely find the best source to tell us why we are here, or, better yet as said in the parlance of our day, 'what life really means.' We look to prophecy as a means to answer life's ultimate questions.

Speaking objectively and in a neutral way, there are a number of considered theories concerning where we may find information disclosing doomsday and its implications regarding the identity of our creator. This 'smart someone' could be the God of the Bible speaking through the Scripture; it could be our human ancestors from many millennia ago who left advice embedded in ancient documents or megalithic artifacts; or it could be extraterrestrials who manage our evolution and pass messages to us in unconventional channels.** The help we seek lies 'beyond' us: It's from (1) God or (2) enlightened individuals in the past or (3) 'from above' whether it's spiritual beings dwelling in another dimension; or friendly spacemen visiting from a nearby region in outer space. In any event, we assume access to such truth is our heritage – be it out of this world or at least out of the ordinary. Therefore, such wisdom makes a big difference in the manner we live our lives. We quickly reckon (because it's far from obvious) if this knowledge exists, it's *encoded*, and we must seek it earnestly if it's to be deciphered.

Underlying this hypothesis rests a staunch belief in purpose. Humankind's presence is no accident. That's why it's only the spiritually minded who eagerly tackle this quest. Should we

---

** I am of course only mentioning this 'God as an alien astronaut' as a possibility, not that I give it equal credence to the other possibilities. *Ancient astronaut theory*, made famous by the writings of Erich von Däniken, is also on the verge of becoming a religion. We see Catholic Priests and a few liberal theologians now choosing to assert that 'God' is actually an extraterrestrial being (s).

discover this information truly exists, *it throws a completely new light on the issue of meaning.*

Consider: What would happen if we uncovered detailed information about the Mayan prophecies distinctly beyond doubt? What if the biblical passages regarding the end time's scenario in fact mirror what happens in the months ahead? What if a spaceship lands on the White House lawn and proclaims that life exists throughout the universe – with radiant alien beings presented as *the living proof*? Furthermore, what if alien life forms inform us (as many 'ancient astronaut theorists' and new age authors have ventured), they have been *caretakers of life here on earth*? Whoever the source is, the important point is *once transcendence has been proven* (something bigger than us exists outside our empirical everyday world); we can bet life will never be the same. Our meaning has a stamp of legitimacy. *Discovering the source provides the means to validate our transcendence.* No doubt, this recognition bestows strong motivation to put our hands to the plow and unearth such evidence.

This doesn't mean the hunt is exclusively a Christian excursion. Quite to the contrary, the religious of most flavors are steadfast in their efforts to uncover whether or not this compulsion concerning the future is warranted. And yet, it is the teaching of Judaism and Christianity that prophecy is the litmus test for which religion comprises ultimate truth. Discovering who knows the future (who can accurately predict what will in fact happen) is the test God sets forth. He asserts:

> *Remember the former things of old: for I am God, and there is none else; I am God, and there is none like me, declaring the end from the beginning, and from ancient times the things that are not yet done, saying, My counsel shall stand, and I will do all my pleasure. (Isaiah 46:9, 10)*

That's why his standard for accuracy is simple: It's 100% right, 100% of the time. There's no room for missing one prophecy. A prophet who predicts something that doesn't come true should be stoned. Deuteronomy 18:20-22 says:

> *But the prophet, which shall presume to speak a word in my name, which I have not commanded him to speak, or that shall speak in the name of other gods, even that prophet shall die.*

> *And if thou say in thine heart, 'How shall we know the word which the LORD hath not spoken?' When a prophet speaketh in the name of the LORD, if the thing follow not, nor come to pass, that is the thing which the LORD hath not spoken, but the prophet hath spoken it presumptuously: thou shalt not be afraid of him.*

Once we settle this question, which religion knows what the future holds, we should pay attention to whatever else the religion holds true.

For believers in the Judeo-Christian concept of afterlife or the Kingdom of God, we suppose our next life will be much better than our life today. Certainly, *we want our problems and pain eliminated by the coming of Messiah.* It may be doomsday for the world, but because we expect salvation, we look forward to the Kingdom of God; we see it as *our solution* and our destiny. Decoding the apocalypse informs us just how soon 'rest from our toils' arrives. Indeed, reassurance grows from remembering this 'rest' lies directly ahead.

Taken to the extreme, this motive becomes irresponsible. As we'll discuss in more detail later, escaping from this life to the next can be ducking out on our responsibilities. It can even prove we lack true faith. But looking forward to the 'City of God'[††] (an historic image representing the New Jerusalem), may reveal our faith. St. Paul says of Abraham, *"For he looked for a city which hath foundations, whose builder and maker*

[††] We likely think of St. Augustine's classic work, *The City of God* which actually focuses on the Church as the community of God.

[is] God." (Hebrews 11:10) And of those who have died in faith looking forward to their future reward: *"These all died in faith, not having received the promises, but having seen them afar off, and were persuaded of [them], and embraced [them], and confessed that they were strangers and pilgrims on the earth... But now they desire a better [country], that is, an heavenly: wherefore God is not ashamed to be called their God: for he hath prepared for them a city"* (verses 13, 16).

The Rapture of the Church is labeled 'the Blessed Hope' precisely because it promises believers will avoid some or all of the Great Tribulation. The Bible commends those who look forward to the return of Christ and for those who seek His Kingdom. For instance, only the *Book of Revelation promises a blessing to those who read it.*

If we take the Bible to be a sacred book, seeking to know the time and seasons offers a reminder to prepare. *"Watch for you know not when the Son of Man comes."* Being watchful demands we keep an eye out for the Master. We do this not because we're afraid to get caught in a regrettable action, but because Jesus admonished His disciples to remain alert. Like the wise virgins in one of Jesus' parables, we're to keep our 'lamps trimmed' and buy extra oil in case the groom of the wedding feast tarries and doesn't show until the wee hours of the morning (Matthew 25:1-12). To do otherwise (as stated in another of Jesus' parables), proves us 'disobedient and foolish servants.' (Matthew 25:14-30).

In summary, seeing prophecy fulfilled in our day reinforces our faith. Later, we will recount how various prophecies were fulfilled in history demonstrating the accuracy of the Bible.

Here my intent is to underscore only that prophecy validates our faith and thus, implies the falsehood of someone else's.[‡‡]

Prophecy fulfilled offers proof that *what we believe* is much more than *wishful thinking*.

FOR FURTHER THOUGHT: Do we value 'proofs' for our faith? Are we aware of the many prophecies in the Old Testament that Jesus fulfilled in his life? What are some of those prophecies? If the prophecy related to the First Advent of Jesus Christ was fulfilled in history, does this argue that prophecy regarding His Second Advent will also be 'historically' fulfilled? Does this make prophecy about His Second Coming 'more certain' because the Bible already has 'gotten it right' in the past? Do we see our faith as a 'fire insurance' package or an umbrella policy? Do we connect the meaning of prophetic truths to their practical application to our daily lives? How does prophecy impact the way we approach the day? Do we proclaim 'Carpe diem'[§§] or, 'Let the carping begin'?

[‡‡] Proving someone else wrong may not be a desirable aspect of seeking to prove ourselves right. But it's an unavoidable consequence if the basic premise of logic is correct: "A is not non-A." Additionally, anticipating the charge of arrogance, Christianity is not intended at its core to be a 'religion' prescribing repetitive behaviors to make one feel worthy or relieved of guilt. Neither is it meant to teach methods to transcend physical reality, to depart into the realm of the spirit, that we might explore sublime experiences or visions. Instead, it intends first to establish a right relationship between God and humankind, one person at a time. Once through that doorway by receiving Christ, Christianity (and Judaism before it), stresses loving God, "with all our heart, soul, and mind" and "loving our neighbor as ourselves." As Jesus said, these are the greatest commandments (See Mark 12:30, Deuteronomy 11:13; 13:3).
[§§] *Carpe diem*, 'Seize the day!'

3: As the End of the World Begins

*But ye, brethren, are not in darkness, that that day should overtake you
as a thief. Ye are all the children of light, and the children of the day:
we are not of the night, nor of darkness. Therefore let us not sleep, as
do others; but let us watch and be sober. For they that sleep, sleep in
the night; and they that be drunken are drunken in the night. But let
us, who are of the day, be sober, putting on the breastplate of faith and
love; and for an helmet, the hope of salvation. For God hath not appointed us to wrath, but to obtain salvation by our Lord Jesus Christ,
Who died for us, that, whether we wake or sleep, we should live together with him. Wherefore comfort yourselves together,
and edify one another, even as also ye do.*
(I Thessalonians 5:4-11)

I T IS A TIMELY SUBJECT: THE END OF THE WORLD. I ADMIT I
FIND THE TOPIC FASCINATING – AND ALWAYS HAVE. WHEN I
WAS ONLY 13, I LEARNED MUCH ABOUT THE TOPIC FROM HAL
Lindsey's *Late Great Planet Earth*. While controversial then
and now, Lindsey's greatest strength was communicating the
themes of 'The Apocalypse' in a conversational and clever
way. Like millions of others who read Hal's book, I was
struck by the fact the current time in which I was living
might be very special. I could conceivably see *the end of the
world!*

What struck me most about what I was reading was, in a
word, *relevance*. My parents had brought me up in the
church and I was, I'm convinced, already a true believer. Like
most good Methodists, my heart had been 'strangely warmed.'
I had 'prayed the prayer of salvation' as a child, very consciously and very sincerely. Thanks to Billy Graham's TV
ministry, I most definitely asked Jesus Christ into my heart.
But, whatever Christianity meant to me, it certainly didn't
seem to connect with the rest of what was happening in the
world.

Enter *The Late Great Planet Earth*. All of a sudden I looked at what was going on in the world in a very different way. This was when war and oil embargoes in the Middle East were center stage. It was bracketed by the 1967 War where Israel regained control of Jerusalem and the 1973 Yom Kippur war in which Israel almost disappeared. Seeing these events and having a best-selling author tie them to the Bible and the predicted *Second Coming of Jesus Christ* was life changing. My worldview would never be the same.

But wasn't I frightened? Hadn't the vision of the end of days made me depressed or cynical? No doubt most kids at 13 or 14 contemplating tumultuous world events would either be bored silly or scared to death. I was different. Far from being frightened, I was excited to watch and see what would happen next. It was like watching pieces of a puzzle fall into place. Watching everyday news confirmed my faith. Plus, I knew things that others didn't know. Following the predictions of the Bible as interpreted by Lindsey (the *dispensational** way as it's known in theology), I could anticipate what might happen next. But most importantly, I could rest assured that God did indeed have "the whole world in his hands." So if some series of world events seemed sure to lead us to nuclear war or to some other form of world destruction, I could compare that scenario against the scenario pitched by Lindsey. And

---

* *Dispensations* in theology are essentially different eras or differing phases of how God interacts with humankind. The two most basic are *Law* and *Grace*. The dispensation of Law essentially proposes that humankind must follow the Law of God to be 'right with God.' The dispensation of Grace declares that while the law of God is Holy and good, only God's Grace allows us any access to God and that God's main course of dealing with people is by His gracious nature. Christians believe that with the death of Jesus Christ on the cross, God's grace now provides access to God's person. Our right standing with God is assured by God's gracious act of dying (through Jesus Christ, God incarnate) on the cross.

since his was the biblical scenario, I knew it must be true and therefore, not to worry about the Russians dropping bombs on us – that just wasn't in the cards, or more properly, in the prophecies of the Bible. Furthermore, before something like that could happen, the followers of Jesus Christ would be suddenly removed from the earth, *"in a moment, in the twinkling of an eye"* (I Corinthians 15:52). The *Rapture* was our assurance Christians wouldn't suffer the worst of bad times.

I remember vividly talking with one of my college history professors in 1974. He was an expert in European history. I made the statement that, according to the Bible, soon the nations of Europe would become a United States of Europe. There would be a common currency, a common parliament, and eventually a common leader. I said these things because of what I'd read in *The Late Great Planet Earth*. My professor could hardly stop laughing. "There is no way that the Europeans could ever unite. They are far too parochial and divided. They always have been and always will be." I said in response, "You watch. My words will come to pass!" Of course, they really weren't my words but the words of the Prophet Daniel and John the Revelator. I suppose I have the last laugh. The reality of this prophetic fulfillment is startling. But it's not the only one I've witnessed in my lifetime.

My brother Phil shared a book with me about a fellow who owned a car wash, the "Diffy Duck Car Wash." The timeframe was around the middle 1980's. I forget the name of the book, but how could I forget the name of his business? This first-time author wrote about an exodus that was coming, according to the Bible, which would make the Jews forget about the Exodus from Egypt. Soon there would be tens of thousands that would be drawn out of countries across the globe (but particularly in Europe) and would immigrate to Israel – "in the last days." The author sought to prepare Christians in Europe to help Russian Jews who would near-term (he predicted) be released from their captivity in the land of the North and make their way back to their homeland. He stressed that Christians should be prepared to take them in as a respite on their way back to the Holy Land.

The book seemed crazy. Additionally, who could take a guy seriously who interpreted a Bible prophecy as a modern soon-to-be historical event, when he ran "The Diffy Duck Car Wash?" But a few years later, when the walls of East Berlin fell, I quickly remembered the car wash man. In 1989 and for the next several years, we watched as thousands and thousands of Jews in the then Soviet Union made their way to Israel. Prophecy was fulfilled once again. I learned a lesson that we should never forget today: *The Bible's prophecies are fulfilled in space-time.* They are much more than mythical stories to make us feel close to God (which is what the modernist theologian supposes). Therefore, we best remember all Bible prophecies, many yet to be fulfilled speaking to the Second Coming, will also be historical events. I'm convinced when we who call ourselves evangelical talk about the *inerrancy* of the bible, or that we take the Bible *literally*, this is really the point we are making. The Bible isn't mythology. It is historical fact. Some of its passages are about past events, *history that has already happened.* But it's also about events in the future, *history that will soon come to pass.* That's why Hebrew prophets set forth their prophetic utterances in *past*, not future tense! It's also why the cliché is so true: Christianity is primarily about *news*, not *views*. The gospel is the 'good news' of Jesus Christ.

Although I believe my thinking is much more mature today, the 'Rapture' perspective – the 'blessed hope' – is still a cornerstone of my faith. I am much better versed in theology forty years later and now I am well aware of how many different ways Scripture can be interpreted. It is by no means a slam dunk that history will play itself out according to the

Dispensational interpretation of the Bible. But the core concept of God saving His righteous ones *in history* is shared by all schools of Christian theology – and indeed Jewish theology as well.[†] History points to a very specific direction with a very special outcome. There are reasons for what happens.

The influence of Christianity explains many aspects of where we find the world today; but one of the most foundational is simply this: Jesus Christ came into our world, lived as a real physical person (not just a *spirit being* as Gnostics and 'New Agers' would argue), and by His death and resurrection altered history arguably more than any other person ever did.

The Christian faith is a *space-time* faith. God created *space-time*. God came into space-time and lived as a human. He was born a baby. He died a real death. When He was resurrected, His resurrected body was witnessed by hundreds of people over several weeks. If television cameras were there, they would have recorded what happened. Cell phones would have taken pictures. *YouTube* would bear witness that the man Jesus was in fact alive after having been executed by the Romans. Even the Apostles challenged the religious rulers opposing them with the quip, "You know about these things... they weren't done in the dark!" (Acts 2:22, paraphrased)

Christianity isn't just about ideas and sentiments. It isn't just about being spiritual and feeling a part of all that is in some mystical or mindful way. Jesus Christ made history – literally. And His teaching is that we as His followers are to 'make history' too – even if it is on a much smaller scale. We are to engage in what happens in our world and make things better,

---

[†] The final Dispensation is known as 'the Millennial Kingdom' in which Christ physically reigns on the earth for 1,000 years, occupying the throne of David, ruling humankind from Jerusalem. Jews refer to it as the Davidic Kingdom.

as much as we can to the best of our abilities. In short, *we are to be relevant.*

When I think about the 'end of the world' I don't think about selling everything and heading to the mountains. That is certainly what many devoted followers of Jesus Christ have done in times past. What is ironic: Such a move is exactly the opposite of what the Second Coming of Christ teaches. Far from giving up and escaping the world, we are to demonstrate how our faith impacts the events of the days we have upon this earth. We are to showcase what the coming Kingdom will be like *by how we treat one another now.* Jesus' imminent return (at any moment) reminds us every day is a 'day of judgment' because what we do in that day is fixed in space and time – it can't be erased. Each day leaves an imprint in the fabric of history. Today may be the only day I have left to make an impact – to make history in my own small way.

FOR FURTHER THOUGHT: Does my life make God seem relevant to the people who know me? Do I consider how important each day is and what happens, from God's perspective, is permanently recorded in space and time? Can I put the past behind me and 'press on to the upward call of Christ Jesus?' Why is it important to stress Jesus was an historical figure and that His death happened in 'space-time'? Is there anything I have done lately that gives others who know me a glimpse of the Kingdom to come? Do I approach each day as a 'day of judgment?'

4: Signs of the Times

The Pharisees and Sadducees came to put Jesus to the test. They asked him to show them a miraculous sign from heaven. He replied, "In the evening you look at the sky. You say, 'It will be good weather. The sky is red.' And in the morning you say, 'Today it will be stormy. The sky is red and cloudy.' You know the meaning of what you see in the sky. But you can't understand the signs of what is happening right now. An evil and unfaithful people look for a miraculous sign. But none will be given to them except the sign of Jonah."
(Matthew 16:1-4, New International Readers Version - NIRV).

"No one knows about that day or hour. Not even the angels in heaven know. The Son does not know. Only the Father knows. Remember how it was in the days of Noah. It will be the same when the Son of Man comes. In the days before the flood, people were eating and drinking. They were getting married. They were giving their daughters to be married. They did all those things right up to the day Noah entered the ark. They knew nothing about what would happen until the flood came and took them all away. That is how it will be when the Son of Man comes." (Matthew 24:36-39, NIRV).

I'M A RECOVERING, 'DVDAHOLIC.' I LOVE MOVIES. ONE OF MY FAVORITES IS JAMES CAMERON'S *TERMINATOR 2: JUDGMENT DAY (1991).* THE MOVIE INTRODUCED SOME OF THE greatest special effects ever seen at the cinema. I'm sure most readers remember the story: Sarah Connor strives to save her son John who represents the one chance humanity has AFTER the world as we know it is destroyed by *Sky Net* and the Terminator machines. The movie portrays a vivid nightmare scenario of a nuclear holocaust producing doomsday. When we think about 'the end of the world,' we can't help but think about horrible images such as we see in Cameron's vision of what may be our fate if the machines take over.

We know climax of history by many names, some biblical and some not: Judgment Day, the Day of the Lord, the Time of Jacob's trouble, Doomsday, the End of Days, the End of Time, the Apocalypse, and of course, Armageddon. Humanity seems to have a deeply rooted sense that the outcome of our story is not a *happy ending*. Something terrible will happen. Whether we turn to the Bible or to science, it seems that disaster and cataclysm awaits. Today, in many current books about 2012, speculation runs rampant that one or more natural disasters loom; thus, these books renew this sense of foreboding.*

The history channel in February of 2009 spent an entire week chronicling the many ways catastrophes could destroy humankind. Throughout the last three months of 2008 and all of 2009 the collapse of the world economy seemed more probable than not. In 2011, we worry about a double-dip recession. Indeed, very few fiscal prophets see much improvement ahead. Whether we are talking economics or politics, if someone predicts an awful event lies just around the corner, we no longer call such a person an *alarmist*; they're a *realist*.

Jesus chided the religious leaders of his day – the intelligentsia of his time – for their failure to understand what was happening to them and their nation. He also warned the common person to be cautious about the future – don't assume life will continue in a state of 'normalcy' (as we might label it today, the 'status quo'). Changes do come. There is no one, no life-force, not even God Himself who guarantees *life as we know it* will continue as is. To paraphrase Jesus' words: "It's just like in the days of Noah... everyone was drinking and eating, marrying and giving in marriage (life as usual), and then

---

* The natural disasters that could wreak havoc upon us include sun storms pummeling the earth and thereby generating monster hurricanes; comets striking us with deadly force; or massive cauldrons (like Yellowstone Park) exploding and sending mountains of volcanic ash into the atmosphere creating a 'nuclear winter effect' destroying most animal and plant life on earth. Moreover, these are only a few of the not-so-pleasant possibilities.

BAM! – the flood came and destroyed everyone and stopped everything they were doing."

Sometimes change is so significant it can be labeled *epochal*.[†] Jesus saw the political conditions of his day and could see the inevitable clash between Jewish nationalism and Roman authority. He could see that the status quo was about to change for the Jewish people forever. He warned the politicians and the people to wake up and realize disaster was pending. His prophecies were very specific: The heart and soul of the Jewish identity, their temple, would soon be destroyed. *"Not one stone will be left upon another"* He told His disciples (Matthew 24: 2). Moses predicted fifteen centuries earlier that one day the Jews would be dispersed throughout the world and no longer enjoy the comfort or familiarity of their homeland or their way of life. As a nation, they would be homeless.

It's particularly noteworthy that Jesus uses two stories, that of Jonah and Noah, to point out how history will soon make a dramatic turn. Generally, theologians want to label Jonah (the prophet swallowed by that big fish) and Noah (who built what appeared an impossibly big boat) as obvious 'mythical' figures, supplying such colorful object lessons. It's most interesting since it suggests Jesus made a big mistake in his quarrel with his opposition. Since Jesus emphasized to the Pharisees the 'stark reality' of the situation, picking these particular stories to reinforce His point should be laughable. It would be like predicting on the front page of the *Wall Street Journal* the US economy is set to crash because Charlie Brown carelessly lost his lunch money in that morning's *Peanuts*. As the scholars say, *it's a non sequitur*.

[†] An *epoch* is the beginning of a period in history that authorities consider significant. An epochal event changes the course of history.

Nevertheless, Jesus uses some of the biggest 'whoppers' of all Bible stories to make His point. If Jesus didn't believe that Jonah and Noah were real historical characters, it would weaken His argument that a national catastrophe was ready to occur. *This polemic says something very special about how Jesus viewed the historicity of the Bible.* However, beyond Jesus testimony that these two colorful figures lived just as the Bible says, He's conveys what many others have taught: *Past events teach us how to predict the future.* "Just like the flood of Noah, another judgment lurks and you religious leaders are too caught up in your self-seeking politics to realize what's about to happen. Read the signs of the times. A change in the 'establishment' is inevitable!"

When the Spanish came to the New World in the 15th and 16th centuries, their disembarking spawned 'the apocalypse' for Native Americans. Within a short span of years, the majority of natives died. Worlds collided. American Indians had no immunity against European diseases. We could examine many such devastating events in our human history and draw the same conclusion. Massive changes happen. When they do, the world is never the same.

The *apocalypse*, in one sense, means much more than a one-time event. Whenever massive change impacts a whole group of people, when their lives are turned upside down, what they experience can be likened to *the end of the world*—certainly, the end of *their world as they know it.*

What seems to be the lesson from these passages in the Gospel of Matthew is simply this: "They should have seen it coming." *Recognizing the signs of the times was in fact the best means to avoid the impending disaster.* Being watchful, being aware of what would soon happen, would have allowed many to escape the coming doom. However, since they chose to remain oblivious to the reality their world would soon come crashing down, the destruction was even more devastating.

Isn't this often the case in our personal lives? We hear tell of accounts where lives that should have been lost, *are miraculously spared.* Death is averted. Afterwards, the usual sentiment is "I will never live my life the same way again... I will appreciate each day because it could be my last." Near-death experiences always teach us how precarious life is; we must relish each day as a gift.

In 67 AD, the Roman general Titus and his army surrounded Jerusalem. Titus, the son of Vespasian (and soon to be Caesar himself), gave the inhabitants of Jerusalem a chance to escape the siege. Christian Jews, heeding the warning of Jesus from 35 years previous, left the city and fled to other Christian communities in neighboring lands. However, both the fervent nationalists as well as piously religious couldn't conceive of how God could allow His eternal City to be destroyed. So they stayed. And Jesus' prediction of the destruction of Jerusalem came to pass exactly as he said. Titus burned the temple to the ground. The Roman armies lifted and separated the stones to find the temple gold which had melted during the fire and seeped between the cracks.[‡] As Jesus said, *not one stone was left upon another.* Within a few more years, the nation of Israel was doused and the land desolate. Their world ended. Before this occurred, to the Jews their temple seemed the stoutest of symbols that their religion and exist-

---

[‡] Recently, it has been authenticated that the gold of the Jewish Temple was actually the financial means by which the Roman Coliseum was built. Outside the Coliseum a placard has been found that declares the Coliseum a gift from Titus, the General of the Army destroying Jerusalem, to his Father, Vespasianus (aka, Vespasian), the Caesar until Titus himself became Caesar in 79 A.D. The placard ties the gold of the Jewish Temple to the completion of the Coliseum.

ence was indestructible. It had withstood the threats by Alexander the Great in the 3rd century BC, Antiochus Epiphanes IV of the Syrians in the 2nd century BC, and the Roman emperor Pompey 60 years before the birth of Jesus Christ. Prior to the act of the Roman Titus, predicting the temple's doom was like predicting, well, the Second Coming of Christ today. Like the Jews, we assume it inconceivable that our world could come to a screeching halt.

Will we experience the 'end of the world' in our lifetime? Most evangelical scholars confidently say we will witness the events associated with the Second Coming of Christ within the new few decades if not sooner. What is irrefutable: Some group of our human brothers or sisters (numbering in the tens of thousands or in the tens of millions), will experience a cataclysm that changes their world forever. Where will we be when that happens? We may hear of it on the news or we may observe it from afar. However, we dare not think, "What happened to them can't happen to us." To be sure, our greatest safeguard is to remember what happened to them *can happen to us*. Destiny awaits all of us.

Christianity is not intended to be a religion characterized by fear. Indeed, quite the opposite is true. It's to be a religion of "faith, hope, and love." No doubt there is a certain 'reality check' we must embrace if we wish to be authentically Christian. As we stated at the outset, we're encouraged to be 'watchful' and on our guard. *"Keep watch! Be careful that no one fools you."* (Matthew 24:4) Christian truth teaches many things, but its lesson of 'Judgment Day' serves as a lasting reminder we mustn't be lulled into a belief that safety and security is an entitlement.

Historians generally agree that if the German church had been on its guard, Hitler would likely never have come to power. Their failure is our warning: We must be constantly vigilant and read the signs of the times lest something similar happen in our land. *Tomorrow could be different than today.* It could be very different indeed.

We should consider how *tomorrow is the offspring of today.* What we do, or don't do, will have repercussions from this point forward.

FOR FURTHER THOUGHT: Does my faith depend upon the status quo? What are the warning signs that the status quo is about to change? Is what I'm doing today giving a false impression to others regarding what I believe? Am I contributing to the status quo? Is our leadership taking us down a path to ruin? Is there anything I can do to avert this outcome? Do we need to prepare for a cataclysm? What could strike our 'necks of the woods?' Are we prepared for this event? If not, what causes our reticence to be ready?

5: Walking and Talking Worthy of Our Vocation

*I therefore, the prisoner of the Lord, beseech you that ye **walk worthy** of the vocation wherewith ye are called (Ephesians 4:1)*

*That ye might **walk worthy** of the Lord unto all pleasing, being fruitful in every good work, and increasing in the knowledge of God; (Colossians 1:10)*

*That ye would **walk worthy** of God, who hath called you unto his kingdom and glory. (I Thessalonians 2:12)*

S O FAR, WE'VE ARGUED WHY CHRISTIANITY IS A DISTINCTLY APOCALYPTIC FAITH, STANDING APART FROM OTHER RELIGIONS IN THE STUDY OF THE FUTURE. AS SUCH IT ANSWERS one of our most cherished quests. By the same token, it allows itself to be proven true or false based upon its prophetic accuracy. Additionally, because it is a 'space-time' faith, Christianity intends to be a highly relevant faith. Even the 'signs of the times' speak to how Christ proclaimed God's incursion in our space-time realm. To further emphasize God's connection to history, Jesus related the stories of Noah and Jonah, the most notorious 'mythical' characters of the Bible, insisting that their historical reality confers many details of coming events.

While many highly regarded religious thinkers in our day espouse the distinction between the hard-core fabric of history and the ethereal nature of spirituality, the God of the Bible as disclosed through Jesus Christ, makes no such epistemological distinction. There is no dichotomy between *truth* in spiritual matters and what we see printed in the news.*

---

* Karen Armstrong's new book, *The Case for God*, argues the wisdom of this premise. Her 'case' however, provides a mere restatement (although supremely eloquent) of what mainline Protestant theology has been saying the better part of the last 60 years.

Given that Christian truth demands it be characterized as "down to earth" in a philosophical sense, we should inquire *"what is the practical value for believing in these things?"* If we believe that Jesus will soon return in our space-time realm, how does this affect us? The point being: Since the apocalypse of Jesus Christ hovers close to the center of Christianity, *this notion should have a vital impact upon our daily lives.*

There is the old joke about two priests talking. One says to the other, "Father John, I've just discovered and it's confirmed: *The Lord is returning tomorrow*! Whatever shall we do?" Father John – somewhat perplexed – replies without thinking, "I don't know. But one thing's for sure. We better look busy."

Certainly one practical conclusion we can draw is simply this: W*e are accountable.* We are to be good stewards. We must remember when 'the Master returns' we are required to give account of ourselves and what we've accomplished. Did we invest our time wisely? Did our stewardship yield a return to the Master? Did we do unto others as if we were doing what we did, unto the Lord? As I write these words, I'm sure the many relevant parables of Jesus come quickly to your mind reinforcing how frequently He taught such things to His disciples.

Jesus never indicated that being His true disciple was an easy task requiring little commitment and no modification to the way we live. He cautioned we must 'count the cost of discipleship.' We must make tough choices. In Luke, Chapter 14:27-33, we read the stark conditions of following Christ:

> *"And whosoever doth not bear his cross, and come after me, cannot be my disciple. For which of you, intending to build a tower, sitteth not down first, and counteth the cost, whether he have sufficient to finish it? Lest haply, after he hath laid the foundation, and is not able to finish it, all that behold it begin to mock him, saying, 'This man began to build, and was not*

able to finish.' Or what king, going to make war against an-
other king, sitteth not down first, and consulteth whether he be
able with ten thousand to meet him that cometh against him
with twenty thousand? Or else, while the other is yet a great
way off, he sendeth an ambassage, and desireth conditions of
peace. So likewise, whosoever he be of you that forsaketh not
all that he hath, he cannot be my disciple."

Becoming a disciple of Jesus Christ requires extensive self-examination. Too often, we aren't challenged to count the cost by messengers of the gospel. After all, didn't Jesus say, *"My yoke is easy and my burden is light" (Matthew 11:30)?* Many preachers sell solace to 'parishioners' for mending broken hearts; some promise prosperity to perk up their hopes and dreams as if "godliness is a means of great gain" (I Titus 6:6). But God's Grace, as Dietrich Bonheoffer diagnosed, is cheapened by such promises. Suffering a martyr's death for his association in several assassination attempts on the life of Hitler, Bonheoffer knew firsthand what the cost of discipleship meant. He died hanging naked with a piano wire wrapped around his neck. And yet, he went to the gallows with such serenity his imprisoned colleagues were astonished.

I could continue to beat this drum, since I believe it worthwhile to underscore our obligation to follow Christ authentically. True, we should admit we've squandered many opportunities – we've failed to follow Christ perfectly. Indeed, we've sinned as the Bible asserts. It's not surprising that the return of Christ causes us to 'clean up our act.' The Bible states that reflecting on the soon coming of Jesus Christ sanitizes our incentive. *"And every man that hath this hope in him purifieth himself"* (I John 3:3). But dwelling on the 'stick' rather than the 'carrot' is not really my style. My inspiration is a positive one. I recognize many constructive benefits from conviction about the Second Coming. There is little need to focus on our failures to heed the Master's call. Christ's coming shouldn't provoke fear we will be found wanting. Consequently, *my focus is on the 'upside.'*

In part, I confess this positive approach owes to my suspicion that many who read this book present a pretty clean act to begin with; not to mention are also well grounded in the knowledge that our salvation depends not upon what we do, but because of *what God has done for us through the death of Jesus Christ on the cross* (Romans 5:8). So then, is there any reason readers who strive to live a consecrated life should bother reading these 'essays'? Obviously, I wouldn't put pen to paper, (metaphorically speaking that is, since I make good use of my word processor), if I didn't believe there was need.

Let me cite several important reasons: We *must adopt the right motives, consider what others see as the message of the gospel as illustrated by the way we live today, refresh our message according to a more thorough and scholarly interpretation of the Bible, and consecrate the time we have left in order to maximize our impact upon the unbelieving world.* These hopeful goals summarize my intent in writing and also serve as a proposal for a sound, albeit abbreviated agenda to follow, as we evaluate ourselves daily.

Why do we need to 'have our wheels realigned?' All too often, those inclined to study prophecy appear compelled for the wrong reasons. Consequently, I propose several questions for our self-examination: "Are we fascinated by the end of the world because it is a scintillating topic? Are we 'code breakers' hoping to finally discover a hidden secret about the nature of the Second Coming of Jesus Christ? Do we believe that the Bible holds a hidden date that tells us exactly when Jesus will return to this earth? Are we depressed about our personal predicament and hoping for an 'out-of-this-world' quick escape?"

Because it affects the way in which we live, it's appropriate – even necessary – to examine why we focus on the subject of prophecy. Moreover, we should question if we have 'gone out of balance' regarding the entirety of the gospel message. There is much more to learn from the Bible than just predictions about the future. While experts point out the Bible devotes 25% of its content to the subject (typically an argument for why we should study prophecy), there is another 75% addressing other topics: Theology, history, how to worship God, and how we should treat one another. Consequently, the challenge to consider is, "Are we so concerned about prophecy that we pay little attention to other matters important in the present day?" We need to balance our learning and our living.

There is an oft quoted cliché how some Christians are "so heavenly minded that they are no earthly good." Are we 'guilty as charged?' Or do we engage in activities underscoring the Love of God and His plan for humankind? Do we understand who our neighbor is? Do we come to his/her aid? Do we defend the doctrine – God created the world and expects us to be its caretakers? Or do our actions present a point of view evincing an unbiblical understanding of our responsibilities (i.e., our stewardship) of this planet? When it comes to matters of 'social justice' – a term often associated with the 'leftish agenda' (and the connotation that 'social justice' is a non-issue for evangelicals) – do we seek support for those put down or repressed? Whether it's a simple case of kids being bullied in school, gang violence in the 'hood,' or the corner grocer run out of business by a national supermarket chain, do we sit on our laurels offering no help?

As Christians, doing 'the right thing' remains our responsibility even if we believe we only have a few months or years left before Christ returns. How we behave morally, ethically, and socially reflects upon who we are and, lest we forget, *who God is.* If we take seriously the message of Genesis that we are image bearers of God, how can we fail to realize our actions communicate louder than words? A tree is known by its fruit.

It's not that these public or civil actions take precedence over our commitment to personal piety, virtue, and evangelism; nonetheless God commands us to "do good works" – it's for this purpose we are called. *"And let us consider one another to provoke unto love and to good works"* (Hebrews 10:24, see also I Timothy 6:18; Titus 3:8, 14). As mentioned earlier, Jesus taught: "We are the salt of the earth" – therefore, we must maintain our 'saltiness.' *"Ye are the salt of the earth: But if the salt have lost his savour, wherewith shall it be salted? It is thenceforth good for nothing, but to be cast out, and to be trodden under foot of men"* (Matthew 5:13).

Consider the story of William Wilberforce (1759 – 1833), a fervent evangelical and the essential catalyst bringing an end to the slave trade in England.[†] The exploitation of slaves was hardly something he could accept in good conscience and sit idly by, doing nothing. His intent glowed pure and consistent with the gospel of Christ. But he was ignored, threatened, and mocked for his witness that slavery must end in England. Whether it was Parliament, the leaders of the Church of England, or successful businessmen (mind you, all 'members in good standing in the Christian Kingdom of England!'), Wilberforce risked his life and health to make a difference. His actions brought enormous change to the world.

The 'full gospel' of Jesus Christ is sometimes associated with the baptism of the Holy Spirit. There is no question that Christians should showcase they live not just on their own power, but through the power of the Holy Spirit – the Spirit of Jesus Christ – living within us. *"For as many as are led by the Spirit of God, they are the sons of God"* (Romans 8:14). Nevertheless, while we are commanded to be filled with the Spirit (Ephesians 5:18), the *fullness of the gospel* means far

---

[†] The movie, *Amazing Grace (2007)*, tells this inspirational story

more than expressing a *supernatural* means enabling a genuinely spiritual life. Each of us is required to "walk a walk" worthy of His calling:

- *I therefore, the prisoner of the Lord, beseech you that ye* **walk worthy** *of the vocation wherewith ye are called (Ephesians 4:1)*

- *That ye might* **walk worthy** *of the Lord unto all pleasing, being fruitful in every good work, and increasing in the knowledge of God; (Colossians 1:10)*

- *That ye would* **walk worthy** *of God, who hath called you unto His kingdom and glory. (I Thessalonians 2:12)*

How we conduct ourselves is proof of God's calling. If we don't walk worthy of His calling, logic leads us to question the legitimacy of our commitment, and therefore, our salvation. *"Brethren, give diligence to make your calling and election sure: for if ye do these things, ye shall never fall"* (II Peter 1:10).

When it comes to 'getting the message of biblical prophecy right' – the next item demanding our attention – I wish to consider in the pages ahead how our traditional language and concepts actually stand up to a thoughtful, fresh, and scholarly review of the Bible. Have we chosen the right words to communicate our convictions? Is our 'witness' for the veracity of biblical prophecy compelling today? Are the 'old words and usual concepts' – what we'd consider tried and true – faithful to the biblical text, so that we convincingly communicate our views? Are our words *relevant* to the world in which we live? This doesn't imply we must change the Bible's message. To the contrary, the Bible's message must be upheld with authority. However, if any 'old way with words' compromises the clarity and truthfulness of the Bible in our world today, such phrases must be retired.

Another way to express this idea: Students of prophetic themes over the years have developed their own language (i.e., jargon) like any other group. Students of prophecy may be guilty of using labels and terms familiar to those of us 'on the inside' but which convey wrongs ideas to those not in the loop. Most of those 'outside our circle' know the word *rapture* but they likely entertain vivid misconceptions about what this event means. When they hear the term *millennium*, they may think 'Millenarians' and immediately assume it references current day apocalyptic advocates selling their possessions and heading to the hills. It's a sad truth that *the craziest of the crazy are typically apocalyptic kooks*. Think Jim Jones, David Koresh, and Charley Manson. For many, believing in the Second Coming infers we are as out-of-touch as those who live in cloistered cults. After all, aren't 'apocalyptics' just like the members of *Heaven's Gate* who committed suicide when the spaceship supposedly following the Hale-Bopp Comet didn't land? To mainline culture, those who believe in the apocalypse are not only foolish, they could become criminal.

If we provide a vivid and correct portrayal of the gospel of Christ by the way we live, our words might seem less important. Nevertheless, both vital deeds and powerful words are imperative. Consequently, we must be aware of the words we use. Are we making 'best efforts' to ensure we are emphasizing the real message of Christ? Or do we obscure His message but 'majoring on the minors?' Too many times, Christians measure spirituality by non-conformity. Indeed, Paul admonishes not to *"be contaminated by the world, but being transformed by the renewing of our minds, so we can prove that God's will is perfect"* (Romans 12:1, 2, paraphrased). We are 'not of this world.' But this phrase is often misinterpreted and an excuse for behaving oddly.

Maintaining a distinction from the world's way of doing things doesn't mean we have to be simpletons. There is no rule that mandates those believing in the return of Christ have to be unsophisticated and uncultured. God's creative impulse is a major aspect of the 'divine image' in us. Few human endeavors can be more sacred than art, poetry, building, or even engineering a new bridge. Creativity, more than cleanliness, is next to godliness. The fact Jesus was a carpenter should be symbol enough. Furthermore, to the extent we achieve seclusion from the world for the sake of piety – we make ourselves and our message inaccessible to others. Our witness may suffer. Cloistered Christians, literally or by liberal use of jargon in our language, cloak the gospel making it more difficult for non-believers to comprehend. Those who haven't come to a saving knowledge of Jesus Christ 'cannot relate' – and we mustn't say it's because they are 'unregenerate men or women' unable or unwilling to hear the message of the gospel.

Finally, as believers who sense the end draws near, it's paramount we prayerfully consider how we live during the remaining time we have on this earth. As the Psalmist said, *"So teach us to number our days, that we may present to You [God] a heart of wisdom"* (Psalm 90:12, *New American Standard Version*).

We are all familiar with the stereotypical doomsday prophet walking the streets hoisting a sandwich board upon his shoulders. The board broadcasts a stark message painted with black paint on the white background: "The End is Near." Some might be critical of this singular demonstration; sizing him up as a laid-off roustabout, typically sporting a long beard and tattered clothes, who *does more harm than good*. But I would propose drawing this conclusion isn't just arrogant – it's patently untrue. It's much more likely this unsavory character just isn't called to testify *to you*.

Furthermore, it begs a related and personally difficult question: While we may not don a disagreeable sandwich board, *"Is our testimony doing more harm than good"*? As believers in Bible prophecy, how we carry ourselves and convey the message that *'The End is Near!'* may be the only warning that many of our family or friends will heed. If so, the question we must ponder is, "Can those to whom God wishes for me to speak take me seriously?" While Bible prophecy and the Second Coming of Jesus Christ may be the most solemn and sobering theme of the calamitous times in which we live, do our lives and words bear witness to it? Certainly, we profess faith and perhaps few would doubt our sincerity. But do we 'transmit' *hope for the future* despite the desperate times? Do we share the love of Christ with others in such a way those around us know we are Christian? Are we making the most of the time remaining? If we practice the evangelical imperative to share our faith with those 'who are without hope' (Ephesians 2:12), we should be encouraged. As times grow more difficult, the door marked "Speaking the words of Christ" opens wider. The Apostle John reminds us the time is short. *"He which testifieth these things saith, 'Surely I come quickly.' Amen. Even so,* **come, Lord Jesus.***"* (Revelation 22:20).

Keeping watch is our foremost responsibility in these last days before the return of the Savior. But note: Keeping watch includes *walking a walk worthy of the vocation to which we've been called.* We can easily see the morning sky is red and the storm heads our direction. Are we prepared? Remember: *Much of our preparation lies in the way we live this very day.* We may emit great words of encouragement and edification. But our lifestyle and our behavior towards others supplies a non-verbal demonstration with even higher decibel levels than any manner of speech. We show our maturity and readiness for the Kingdom. Or we illustrate just the opposite. It's time we take a self-assessment to determine which outcome best reflects who we are.

FOR FURTHER THOUGHT: Do we feel intimated by the requirement that we walk a walk worthy of God's calling?

What does it mean for us to count the cost of discipleship? When you think of individuals who have counted the cost, to whom do your thoughts go? Jesus said that "He who does not lay down His life for my sake is not worthy of Me" (Matthew 10:38). Do we find areas of our lives that we must 'lay down' to become worthy of Christ? What is holding us back? Are creating works of art worthy ways to spend our time? Do we estimate that persecution for our beliefs lies ahead? Do we feel motivated to talk to those we love about 'the hope that is within us?' If we find we are unable, what obstructs our path?

6: The Prince Who Brings Peace

*For unto us a child is born, unto us a son is given: and the government
shall be upon his shoulder: and his name shall be called Wonderful,
Counselor, The mighty God, The everlasting Father, The Prince of Peace.*
(Isaiah 9:6)

*Then the same day at evening, being the first day of the week, when the
doors were shut where the disciples were assembled for fear of the Jews,
came Jesus and stood in the midst, and saith unto them, Peace be unto
you. And when he had so said, he shewed unto them his hands and his
side. Then were the disciples glad, when they saw the LORD. Then said
Jesus to them again, Peace be unto you: as my Father hath sent me, even
so send I you. And when he had said this, he breathed on them, and saith
unto them, Receive ye the Holy Ghost: Whosoever sins ye remit, they are
remitted unto them; and whosoever sins ye retain, they are retained. But
Thomas, one of the twelve, called Didymus, was not with them when Jesus came. The other disciples therefore said unto him, We have seen the
LORD. But he said unto them, Except I shall see in his hands the print of
the nails, and put my finger into the print of the nails, and thrust my
hand into his side, I will not believe. And after eight days again His disciples were within, and Thomas with them: then came Jesus, the doors being shut, and stood in the midst, and said, Peace be unto you. Then saith
he to Thomas, Reach hither thy finger, and behold My hands; and reach
hither thy hand, and thrust it into My side: and be not faithless, but believing. And Thomas answered and said unto him, My LORD and my God.
Jesus saith unto him, Thomas, because thou hast seen Me, thou hast believed: blessed are they that have not seen, and yet have believed.*
(John 20:19-29).

IN THE NORTHERN PART OF ISRAEL IS A VALLEY CALLED ME-
GIDDO. KNOWN BY MANY NAMES IN THE BIBLE, IT IS PRINCI-
PALLY REMEMBERED FOR THE "MOUNTAIN OF MEGIDDO,"
Har-megiddon, or the more common English spelling, *Armageddon*. The mere use of the name evokes images of war and
massacre, of nuclear devastation and vast armies destroying
one another. Armageddon is a frightening concept and the
very word itself has become a common label for the world's
destruction no matter what the cause.

For decades apocalyptics have used such frightening images as a means to impress upon others the nearness of the 'battles to end all battles.' There are many fervent voices proclaiming the upcoming destruction and death. Because I am an evangelical Christian who also believes in the Second Coming of Jesus Christ, I pay careful attention to this talk. At times it alarms me. This is not because I personally fear experiencing this great tribulation firsthand. Rather, my discomfort lies in the fact that those of us who fervently believe in the Second Coming may be guilty of overemphasizing these negative images and fearful thoughts. Because we believe that God is a God of love and His most important work in our lives is saving us from the consequences of sin and judgment, I am concerned that we evangelicals may be too preoccupied with dark images and even perseverating on political and militaristic matters in the Middle East to the exclusive of other vital topics.

As believers in Christ's soon return, there is no doubt that beneath our captivation lurks our conviction that the predicted final conflict is brewing. Evangelicals have been taught to be on the lookout for we know not when the Lord will return. But more than this, evangelicals who study their Bibles and listen to evangelical teaching regularly have been immersed in 'the prophetic scenario' of specified world events that signal the alarm – war in the Middle East means Christ is coming soon! We are likely to assume that the battles raging today will trigger Armageddon. (And we're probably right!)

However, because we link these various concepts, it's not uncommon for criticism to be directed our way from unbelievers. It appears to those outside our fold that we hope for the worst, so as the wars increase in frequency and intensity, we can fast-forward to the day of Christ's return. We are criticized for seeking 'the great escape' we know as the 'Rapture.' This event ensures 'the elect' won't experience the terrors of judgment.   It isn't true, but to the outside world, it looks like we don't care if the world 'goes to hades in a handbag.'

I confess I stay tuned in to what's transpiring in Israel and grow more and more convinced that Armageddon is at the door.   But, as I've said above, this outlook unsettles me and makes me wonder if I am thinking about Christ's soon return the right way.   This apprehension becomes obvious when I reflect upon the essential nature of Christ's message to His Church and what it should mean to all believers in our world today.   After all, isn't Christ *"The Prince of Peace?"*

Revelation 16:16 specifically states the location of the final battle. *"Then the evil spirits gathered the kings together. The place where the kings met is called Armageddon in the Hebrew language."*   There can be little doubt the Scripture teaches a war is coming that will make all other wars pale in comparison.   This war will cause spectacular changes.   Even the sun and moon will lose their light and stars will grow dim.

So should I really be uneasy about the preoccupation with violent images in prophecy preaching?   Why do I care that evangelicals who believe as I do about how Christ will return to this earth seem so obsessed with *"wars and rumors of wars?"*   Isn't the impending death and destruction implied by Armageddon a valid means to promote the gospel?

Yes, this approach is simply 'telling it like it is.'   Nevertheless, I worry that many of us who call ourselves evangelicals have become too fixated with the Middle East conflict and unbalanced in our presentation of the gospel message.   Our story must stay balanced.

This awareness dawned on me when listening to Iran's President Mahmoud Ahmadinejad.   Often he is quoted calling for Moslems worldwide to do whatever it takes, including engaging in nuclear war, to literally incite the coming of the Moslem Messiah, the Twelfth Imam or *Mahdi*.   Ahmadinejad is actually making the logical argument we evangelicals are accused of –wishing for the worst in order to provoke the ultimate good to burst forth. This appears to be Iran's key motivation as it pursues its program to build a nuclear weapon. Iran's intention transcends the destruction of Israel – it's an attempt to force the Mahdi out of hiding.

Given *radical* Islam's preoccupation with killing infidels and sponsoring Jihad, isn't this pathway perfectly logical for Islamic Fundamentalists? It would seem so. If 'outing' the Mahdi is what they really wish to pursue, the only reason they haven't gone forward with this plan must be they simply don't yet have the capability. It's much less likely that the reason radical Muslim's haven't consummated this strategy is an unconscious admission that they could be wrong about their beliefs.

But can *orthodox* Christians adopt this tactic? If we are being true to our faith, shouldn't we likewise 'go all in' and do everything we can to encourage Armageddon to happen as soon as possible? When an average person listens in to a prophecy pundit on the TV (of which I have become one!) they generally draw this conclusion. They assume, "Evangelicals who believe in the Pre-Tribulation Rapture of the Church and the Second Coming of Christ are war mongers!" Surely we chafe at this accusation.

Indeed, for the followers of Jesus Christ, it doesn't take much analysis to realize just how wrong-headed such a notion is. During His earthly life, Jesus may not have been a pacifist and may not have opposed all manner of violent resistance to evil. Yet, His words can easily lead to this conclusion. The broad brush strokes of His message challenge us to articulate so-called 'just wars' very carefully. Non-violence seemed to be a key element of his politics. Let's remember: Jesus didn't call for Jihad against the Romans. He didn't put his enemies 'to the sword.' He counseled to *"turn the other cheek"* when struck. He proclaimed that those who *"live by the sword die by the sword."* He indicated that if He were of "this world" His followers would fight. But He is not of this world. So His followers aren't engaged in insurrection. When He appeared after His death, there was no hint that it was 'time to get even.' His approach was not 'an eye for an eye.'

Because our Messiah's post-resurrection admonition was *"May peace be with you,"* it's obvious we should have nothing in common with radical Islam. Islam calls for Jihad against its enemies. Christianity calls for peace and going the second mile to avoid war with our enemies (if at all possible).* But do we convey this outlook convincingly?

Christ called for the creation of a different kind of world. The watch word of His preaching was "The Kingdom of God." His greatest sermon as recorded in the *Gospel of Matthew* explains what the Kingdom of God will be like and how its subjects must conduct themselves. Jesus' message was indeed drastically different from the Judaism of His time. His whole notion of Messiah was not primarily about the Christ who conquers Israel's enemies but a Christ who challenges individuals to get their hearts right with God. His mission was to undergo crucifixion. This was *the* means to salvation. He did not seek to save Israel through a military crusade. The political activists of His time, the Zealots, were very much like the fundamentalist Muslims of today wishing to foment insurgency in order to force the hand of the Almighty. "Send the Messiah, banish the Romans and set up the Kingdom." The shouts of "Hosanna!" are rightly translated as "Save us NOW!"

---

* I do believe in 'just wars' and that God did order his people into battle in the Old Testament – just for the record.

But such deliverance wasn't to be. Jesus couldn't have underscored this any stronger than choosing to ride into Jerusalem on a donkey, a symbol of humility, rather than a white horse. Martin Luther King and Mahatma Gandhi, among many others, portray in modern times that violence and war have nothing to do with Jesus' message or His methodology as He expressed it in the New Testament.

Now, my evangelical brothers who likewise proclaim the nearness of Christ's return might counsel me that I am confusing the First Coming of Christ with the Second. His first appearance was meant to be as 'the lamb of God,' willing to die for us, speaking not a word in His defense, undeterred from suffering vicariously to redeem us from sin. But his Second Coming is different. He will come with His Saints – His mighty ones – all riding on white horses and destroying the Antichrist and the Devil with the Sword of His Mouth. Mind you, *I whole-heartedly agree with this picture.*

Yet, the Scripture clearly teaches that both pictures of the Messiah are accurate. This recognition is perhaps the most essential issue separating Judaism and Christianity. The Messiah doesn't come once, He comes twice: Once as the suffering servant, a second time as the conquering Christ. *Nothing is more central to the Christian interpretation of the Bible (to the contradistinction with the Jewish view) than this point.*

No, I don't think that confusing Christ's First Coming with His Second Coming is my problem. Indeed, I share in the enthusiasm and anticipation of the return of the LORD. As I said earlier, Christ's promised return brings meaning to history and especially to 'my history.'

No, my problem is quite different. Simply put: My conviction is that *we may not be proclaiming Christ's message in a biblical way, consistent with how Jesus presented His Gospel.*

In our eagerness to warn the unbelieving world that judgment is coming, we can't help but preach how events are aligning to the Bible's predicted scenario at the time of Christ's return. The fulfillment of Bible prophecy does reinforce the supernatural character of the Bible and the reality that God is right in the middle of our world today. Furthermore, it demands we communicate to everyone we can why they must make a decision regarding the claims of Jesus Christ immediately. Time is neither on our side nor theirs. This motivation – seeking the salvation of others for their benefit – is proper and praiseworthy.

However, I propose we have mixed motivations. This alternative motivation isn't so worthy. In our eagerness to point out prophetic fulfillment, we may be seeking to overcome what sociologists call, *cognitive dissonance*. This is the behavior exhibited by those who feel their beliefs threatened. When believers begin to doubt, they seek to reinforce their faith primarily for their personal peace of mind. If we are primarily motivated to reassure ourselves of His soon coming, we may find we overemphasize the negative and underemphasize the positive. We latch on to all sorts of *proofs* even if they are at odds with God's authentic message. Let me explain further.

We misstep when we place our desire to confirm our faith before the priority of preaching the right message. To say it another way, citing 'the signs of the times' may be driven by an inner need to prove to ourselves we are on the right track. Looking for signs which prove we are in the final days may be due to our own failure of faith. It's exciting and reassuring seeing prophecies come true. But it's also too easy to read into events and see things that aren't really there as a means to master our doubt. This is especially wrong when we obsess on destructive images hoping that in them we confirm Bible prophecy is coming to pass and our belief is well-placed. We must take a step back and reflect on the fact that when Christ comes into our lives, His presence is to bring peace and put an end to conflict. This is true personally and it's certainly what the promise of His return ultimately means to the world.

When Jesus appeared to His disciples after His resurrection, he "did many signs" to demonstrate He was indeed the Jesus whom they loved. His goal was to make the foundation of their faith *rock solid.* To Thomas he even said, *"Touch the holes in my hands and put your fingers into my side, doubt no longer but believe."* But His goal was much more than offering proofs of His resurrection. Once convinced, the disciples were sent to the world to preach the good news of salvation. That's why we shouldn't become preoccupied with signs. Ultimately, 'proving our point' misses the point. Signs engendering faith are only the beginning. Recall Thomas was chided for demanding to see the holes in Christ's hands and touch the wound in His side. *"Then Jesus told him, 'Because you have seen me, you have believed. Blessed are those who have not seen me but still have believed.'"*

As followers of Jesus Christ, we are responsible to learn His teaching, to center ourselves on that teaching, and to reflect it as accurately as we can. His teaching is primarily salvation – not just for the hereafter but for the 'here and now.' Jesus saves and keeps on saving. Part of that salvation is bringing peace in the worst of times. Not once, but every day.

When the turmoil of our today scares us all the way down to our stockings, it's important we turn to Christ who can bring us peace – not to images of impending doom, but to the assurance that God will bring us peace no matter what the calamity. This doesn't mean He will eliminate the cause of our stress or worry. But it does mean in the midst of our anxiety, we can find the calm. We are even reminded to slow down and take time to rediscover the inner strength God supplies.

"For thus saith the Lord GOD, the Holy One of Israel; In re-turning and rest shall ye be saved; in quietness and in confidence shall be your strength" (Isaiah 30:15).

In John's retelling of Jesus' appearance to His disciples, three times John tells us that Jesus proclaimed *"May peace be with you!"* Peace was the first word out of His mouth. Repeating himself thrice may mean a number of things symbolically; but at the very least it means Jesus wanted His followers to experience a calmness that overcomes calamitous circumstances.

What is the abiding comfort of the soon return of Christ? It is the bringing of peace which comes with the coming of the Kingdom of God. There is no denying that the birth of the Kingdom will be like childbirth. There will be great pain. But on the other side of that pain will be great joy. Evangelicals who believe in the soon return of Christ must keep the *promise of peace at the center of their message.* We must be careful to place the battles and the disasters in their proper context. God is in control. The world will devise countless methods to destroy our peace, but God will ultimately overcome this and bring us to a time of rest. That is the message we must proclaim. It's the message which must influence our lives and be a source of strength to those we know and love. We must be sure our message is not misunderstood.

When Jesus came the first time, angels proclaimed, "Peace on earth and good will toward men." When Jesus comes a second time, He will set in motion a lasting peace that angels and humanity both will proclaim and experience for time and eternity. There's no question, before peace comes the Lord will execute judgment against His enemies. He will destroy them by the breath of His mouth. But lest we be seen to be vengeful ourselves, we should contemplate the calm that He brings after the storm, not just the storm itself. The Prince of Peace would expect nothing less from us.

FOR FURTHER THOUGHT: **When I find myself in turmoil and conflict, can I remember that one of Jesus' greatest gifts to me is the gift of peace? When I consider the Second Coming, do I focus on the images of destruction or the prospect for peace that is promised thereafter? What steps must I take to find peace in the midst of chaos? How can we speak about an eternal peace that is coming when chaos must come first? Are peacemakers today who strive for peace in the Middle East, acting in accordance to Jesus' proclamation, "Blessed are the peacemakers..."?**

7: *Parousia* – The Second 'Presence' of Jesus Christ

*Now we beseech you, brethren, by the **coming** (parousia) of our lord Jesus Christ, and by our gathering together unto him, that ye be not soon shaken in mind, or be troubled, neither by spirit, nor by word, nor by let-ter as from us, as that the Day of Christ is at hand. Let no man deceive you by any means: for that day shall not come, except there **come** (er-chomai) a **falling away** (apostasia) first, and that man of sin **be re-vealed** (apokalyptō), the son of perdition; who opposeth and exalteth himself above all that is called god, or that is worshipped; so that he as god sitteth in the temple of god, shewing himself that he is god. Remem-ber ye not, that, when I was yet with you, I told you these things? And now ye know what withholdeth that he might **be revealed** (apokalyptō) in his time. For the mystery of iniquity doth already work: only he who now letteth will let, until he be taken out of the way. And then shall that wicked **be revealed** (apokalyptō) whom the lord shall consume with the spirit of his mouth, and shall destroy with the **brightness of his coming** (parousia).*
(II Thessalonians 2:1-10)

C HRISTMAS TIME IS THE FAVORITE TIME OF YEAR FOR MANY OF US. AS AN ADULT I HAVE THE ADVANTAGE OF MANY YEARS OF EXPERIENCE THAT ENABLE ME TO ANALYZE THE past and interpret not only its meaning, but in particular what certain events meant to me. Christmas is a time to reflect on the past in order to recreate the best of the past in the present. Just like in Dickens' *Christmas Carol*, there is far more em-phasis on 'Christmas past' than there is on the present or even the future. There are many lessons to be learned from Christmases long ago.

As a child, I was the youngest of four boys. My mother was the youngest of eleven children while my father was the youngest of four brothers. Having so many Uncles and Aunts, I had 23 first cousins. We had a big family. With so many uncles, aunts, cousins, and in some cases, second cousins, our

Christmases were raucous events indeed. We opened most all of our gifts on Christmas Eve and for some crazy reason we had to watch each person open his or her gifts one person at a time. It would lead to a five-hour long exposition of beautifully wrapped packages torn asunder throughout the evening (and into the wee hours of the morning). The youngest went first, the oldest last. Thank goodness for that. At least the kids didn't have to sit through the entire session. For the adults, it was a test of loving endurance to be sure!

Someone has said, "Families are like fudge. They are mostly sweet, but still there are a few nuts." My family, probably like yours, fits this description perfectly. But in my innocence of youth, I didn't realize that any of my relatives had any oddities at all. They were family. And when they gathered together, I was surrounded by people that for the most part loved one another and genuinely valued family as perhaps the most important element of their lives. The partaking of gifts, good food, candy, cakes, and all that goes with the American Christmas, made an indelible impression upon me. In looking back, I realize that our surroundings were actually very modest. We weren't well-to-do. But we were warm, well clothed, and had plenty to eat. As such, my memories are chock full of genuine experiences of joy.

So much of Christmas for kids is about anticipation. We can't wait to open gifts, to attend a parade, to go to the department store, to see Santa Claus. Given that these events were all tied to the gathering of the family, much of my anticipation was directed to those last couple of days before Christmas when we and my many relatives would travel from across Texas and Oklahoma to one of my aunt's houses (or in some seasons to our house!). When the family arrived, all heaven was ready to break loose! It wasn't just about the moment of their arrival. That was usually the most awful of times. I had to kiss my aunts! But immediately after, everyone was together. Candy

came out of the back seat of the cars to be piled high on kitch-
en counters for easy access. Food was put on the stove and
the house smelled like a party all afternoon and night. Feeling surrounded by people, laughter, food, music, and perhaps
football on the television, I was ecstatic. There might even be
wrestling matches with my older cousins right in the middle
of our big living room next to a Christmas tree half-covered-
up by a mountain of presents. It was an intense experience of
contentment and good times.

So what does all of this have to do with the haunting verse
with which I began? Actually, quite a lot.

Christians have always been taught to anticipate the *coming*
of Jesus Christ, a second time. We talk about the Second
Coming, His Second *Advent*, and we connect this phrase to
those cataclysmic events that transpire just before and during
His arrival. But what got me to thinking about the different
ways of 'arriving upon the scene' was carefully considering the
different verbs for 'coming' used in this particular passage of
scripture and several others related to it.

The context of this second letter to the saints at Thessalonica
was Paul's need to express clearly when the time of the Lord's
'coming' would be. And it's intriguing how he talks about the
coming of someone else that must precede the coming of Jesus Christ. This second personage is of course the character
we know as 'the Antichrist.' Before Jesus comes, Antichrist
must come. Paul is saying to his church, "Stop worrying. We
can't yet be living in the time we've called 'the day of the Lord'
because the Antichrist has not yet come."

Paul states that the Antichrist, the son of perdition, can only
come (*erchomai*) after a "falling away" (*apostasia* - apostasy)
comes first. The verb translated **come**, *erchomai*, is frequently used in the New Testament and it has a simple meaning. It means to "come or go" or "make an appearance." It

has a temporal sense, such as, "one event came right after another." For instance, the Three Kings *erchomai* (are come) to worship the Christ child (Matthew 2:2). They **came** from the east (probably Babylon) to Jerusalem.

Likewise, the *apostasia* will come about at a specific moment in time. What is *apostasia*? This word is used in Greek to label "a rebellion, a revolt, a falling away" such as in a state of lawlessness representing a departure from 'law and order' or from orthodoxy in belief. The message is thus, "the Antichrist can only make his appearance at a moment in time in the future after first there *comes to pass* a rebellion or time of lawlessness."

What is more, Paul expresses the distinction of the coming of the Antichrist and Second Coming of Christ by using two different Greek words to signify the nature of their respective 'comings.' These two words are quite different from one another. As to the Antichrist's actual 'coming' Paul expresses it as an *apocalyptō*. Three times he refers to the Antichrist's coming with this term. This 'coming' is much more involved that merely 'showing up' as is expressed in *erchomai*. One can't help but notice it's from the same root word as the word *apocalypsis*, which is the word we translate, **apocalypse**. John's Revelation is an *apocalypsis*. It's a noun that represents 'the full story' of Jesus Christ's manifestation.

But Antichrist's revealing is an *apocalyptō*. "That man of sin (can only) be revealed" (*apocalyptō*) after the apostasy (*apostasia*) has first come to pass. Furthermore, this apostasy is so significant and unique it can only happen after *something is first taken out of the way*. Paul says, *"And now ye know **what** withholdeth that he (Antichrist) might **be revealed** (*apokalyptō) in his time."* Unfortunately for us, we don't know with certainty to *what* or to *whom* Paul was referring. Is the "what" that withholdeth or restraineth this son of perdition, "the law," "the government that maintains order," or as evangelicals mostly believe *the Holy Spirit*, who indwells believers?" Paul goes on to reinforce his assertion: *"For the mystery of iniquity doth already work: only he who now letteth will let, until he be taken out of the way."* Who is this *"he* that must first be taken out of the way?" As many students of prophecy know, this verse deserves its own examination because the doctrine of the Rapture of the Church is closely connected to it. It's no small matter to tackle. Consequently, we will leave this question for another time.

"And then shall that wicked (one) **be revealed** *(apokalyptō) whom the lord shall consume with the spirit of his mouth."* For the third time, Paul uses this word, *apokalyptō*. In each usage, Paul is conveying that the revealing is like an 'unveiling.' Something heretofore has remained hidden and unidentified. It's 'behind the curtains.' But there will be a moment when Antichrist 'comes.' His coming is like a revelation, a surprise, something unexpected. The curtains will suddenly be pulled back. Just like in a magic trick there is a 'reveal.' Like any surprise or trick, once the surprise is revealed, it's no longer a surprise. Whatever the 'shock value,' it wears off in a matter of time. Once the moment passes, it's over and done.

This is the nature of the coming of the Antichrist. It is sudden, it is shocking, and it is unexpected. But, the coming of the Antichrist isn't permanent. It lasts for a short period of time. It is transitory. His time is limited. The Bible says he will cause unparalleled trouble for 3 and one-half years. Then Jesus will come and end Antichrist's time on this earth.

But the word that Paul uses to express the coming of Jesus Christ is quite a different word. The word used is *parousia* (pronounced, par-row-see-a). It's used 24 times in the New Testament and it conveys a very different type of 'coming.' It's a method of coming that just doesn't happen and then it's finished. It is singled out as the word which refers to the Second Coming or Advent of Jesus Christ. When Jesus comes, *he stays. His presence persists.* He sets up His Kingdom and continues on from that moment in time forward. The word *parousia* is a type of *coming* that once it happens it never ends. It's as if the word signifies "when the Lord comes He will never go away again." Furthermore, when He is present, there is no mistaking him. When He arrives on the scene, His presence will be felt from that moment forward. But it's not just about His presence. "Now we beseech you, brethren, by the **coming** (*parousia)* of our lord Jesus Christ, and by our gathering together unto him..." From its first usage, the point of the coming of the Lord is the community that is formed. We are to be "gathered together until him." Once we are united, we will never be separated ever again.

In Vine's New Testament Dictionary, we are told, *parousia* is a noun composed of two words, literally a presence – "*para*" (with) "ousia" (being) (from *eimi,* the verb, "to be") that: "...denotes both an 'arrival' and a consequent 'presence with.'" For instance, in a papyrus letter, a lady speaks of the necessity of her *parousia* in a place in order to attend to matters relating to her property there. Paul speaks of his *parousia* in Philippi, (see Philippians 2:12, in contrast to his *apousia,* "his absence...")... *Parousia* is used to describe the presence of Christ with His disciples on the Mount of Transfiguration, (II Peter 1:16). When used of the return of Christ, at the Rapture of the Church, it signifies, not merely His momentary 'coming' for His saints, but His **presence** with them from that moment until His revelation and manifestation to the world. Parousia is all about 'being with' someone. When Jesus Christ comes, the inference is that He is coming to be with us, personally, and to abide with us forever.

That's what it meant to me for my relatives *to come* to our house for Christmas. This was the anticipation so deeply felt when I was wishing for Christmas. It meant 'being together' and being surrounded by the ones you love and that love you.

Looking for the Second Coming of Christ should be like that for Christians. Christmas time is the season of Advent. Advent is a noun derived from the Latin verb *advenio*, **to come** or **to arrive.** During the season of Christmas, the *coming of Christ* is what we anticipate and celebrate.

Perhaps the oldest Christmas hymn, from the 8th century, is *"O come, O come, Emmanuel."* The hymn is not only a prayer of anticipation, but a song of rejoicing. Emmanuel has come. "Rejoice! Rejoice!" The song says, Emmanuel (which just so happens to mean, "God is with us") has paid the ransom for captive Israel (and for you and me!). Advent isn't just a reminder that Christ came, but that Christ will come again. And when He comes again, He will be with us forever. He will never again leave us. We will be gathered together with Him and with one another. That is why the coming of Christ and the Rapture of the church are to be great words of comfort that we are to express to one another frequently and to remind one another that when He comes again, it will be like Christmas every day of the year, for time and for eternity!

FOR FURTHER THOUGHT: Do I take comfort in knowing that when Christ returns, I will feel His presence and the presence of those I love surrounding me continually? Do I look forward to this time? When I reflect on loved ones already passed, do I rejoice thinking about seeing them again? Does this belief encourage me today? When I think about death, can I conceive of how this biblical truth can restore my faith and give me courage to face death?

8: Heaven on Earth

*Yet have I set my king upon my holy hill of Zion. I will declare the decree:
the LORD hath said unto me, Thou art my Son; this day have I begotten
thee. Ask of me, and I shall give thee the heathen for thine inheritance, and
the uttermost parts of the earth for thy possession. Thou shalt break them
with a rod of iron; thou shalt dash them in pieces like a potter's vessel.*
(Psalm 2:6-9)

*Behold the man whose name is The BRANCH; and he shall grow up out of
his place, and he shall build the temple of the LORD: Even he shall build
the temple of the LORD; and he shall bear the glory, and shall sit and rule
upon his throne; and he shall be a priest upon his throne: and the counsel
of peace shall be between them both.*
(Zechariah 6:12-13)

*And the glory of the LORD came into the house by the way of the gate
whose prospect is toward the east. And he said unto me, Son of man, the
place of my throne, and the place of the soles of my feet, where I will dwell
in the midst of the children of Israel for ever, and my holy name, shall the
house of Israel no more defile*
(Ezekiel 43:4, 7)

MY FATHER HAS A HABIT OF REPEATING HIMSELF. THIS
ISN'T DUE TO HIS AGE. EVEN AT 91 HE IS LUCID AND A
GOOD CONVERSATIONALIST.   TRUE, HIS HEARING
could be better. But he is still a very smart man and comes
across that way to those that are fortunate enough to engage
him in dialogue.

But he has repeated himself for as long as I remember. Most
of us have a fear of repeating ourselves to the boredom of our
friends and family. We may say, "I've probably told you this
before." Or if it's a joke we'll say, "Stop me if you've heard this
one." This isn't my father's fear. I can't recall him fearing
saying the same thing twice (or countless times). Why this
behavior? What appears to motivate his propensity to be repetitive is his desire to reflect on his favorite subjects and es-

pecially insights into life that he cherishes. One of his favorites is his proclamation that we could enjoy heaven on earth if evil people were simply banished and Mother Nature would be a bit better-behaved. "You know," he would counsel me, "if this world were just free of bad people doing bad things, this world would be a great place. It's a beautiful world. It would be heaven enough if it were only this world without the evil that we too often see." My father would then get a distant look in his eyes as if he could visualize such a world and dream of himself living in its midst. It was as if he was hearing *Satchmo** singing, "And I say to myself, it's a wonderful world."

There was a time when I tried to tell him that according to my interpretation of the Bible, he should feel assured such an earth was exactly what 'the Good Lord' (his favorite appellation for our Father in Heaven) has in store for us when Jesus returns. I would try to explain that most evangelicals these days are 'Pre-millennialists' and we believe exactly what he wishes for. Jesus Christ will return to this earth to save it from destruction and then begin a restoration of its beauty. Those who have believed in Him over the past 2,000 years will return too atop white horses (now that will be a 'ride!') After Jesus Christ dispenses with the archenemy of the Bible, *the Antichrist,* Christ will turn his attention to establishing his capital city in Jerusalem and will literally reign on an earthly throne in Israel for 1,000 years (hence this epoch is called the *Millennium*). The Messiah Jesus is to rebuild the Temple and reign on His throne in that very place. When responding to my dad, I would try to explain that *'heaven' will come to earth*, metaphorically speaking. Earth becomes 'paradise restored' (as John Milton might say). When Jesus returns, the earth will be made right. The creation will be refreshed. We

---

* This nickname belongs to Louis Armstrong, for the musically challenged.

will live in peace on this planet. The troubles of the past will be no more. As Isaiah said, *"He shall wipe away every tear"* (Isaiah 25:8 paraphrased). That's what the verses at the beginning of this essay affirm. The Messiah reigns on this earth.

As a bonus, those of us that return with Christ will be transformed into new creatures, no longer mortal, but immortal. We will be co-regents with him and will serve him every day in this wonderful renewed world. We won't fear death or illness. We will be empowered in more ways than we know to handle our new responsibilities of reigning with Christ in His Kingdom.

Now, understand, my father wasn't guilty of ignoring me. Nevertheless, about once a year, starting about 30 years ago, he would find an occasion to remind me of his dream and hope for our world. I would once again try to explain that his insight was right on target and articulate in detail why good, biblical interpretation confirms his hopes. I thought it would add to his delight if he understood his perspective could be backed up by the Bible.

But eventually I came to realize that my father didn't really want a biblical justification for his dream. He didn't want me to explain the difference between Pre-millennialism and Post-millennialism. Such technical distinctions (important though they be!) were lost on him. My sense was that Dad just wanted to ponder such sweet images and enjoy thinking about the future in such a world. This prospect was enough for him. Perhaps the point is my father could visualize 'heaven on earth' and he found in that concept comfort to dissuade doubts about the future and overcome the daily images of deplorable human acts. Thinking about how earth could be transformed into heaven was a powerful coping mechanism. Marx may have thought that believing in heaven was an opiate for the people, to keep them happy while being alienated from their work. But no doubt my dad would tell Marx he was clueless to the satisfaction and confidence it provides believers in Jesus Christ to have unswerving faith in the future life.

Like most of us, my father may have conjectured about the afterlife. We all wonder about its characteristics. Our minds are flooded with unbiblical concepts about heaven and life after death thanks to false religions, classical mythology, and television programs that have mediums and ghosts becoming perpetual characters without much shock value.   Indeed, ghosts are becoming a supernatural means to console or even protect us.   Furthermore, mediums are solving crimes and whispering so-called truths about life's meaning. The supernatural is becoming commonplace. But what is the truth about the nature of the afterlife? What might the afterlife be like? What does biblical prophecy teach us about the future heaven and earth?

For Christians, there is a lot more to it than we generally suppose. Granted, you may be like my father and find the details unnecessary. It's enough to just know that Jesus promises eternal life to those that trust in Him. Perhaps all you need is the promise that death isn't the end. If that is enough for you, you are privileged. Unfortunately for me, I am more than curious concerning what comes next. I want to know about it in detail if you please!

When we study the Bible, it becomes clear that there are four 'phases' of the afterlife. I won't get into the differences between 'Old Testament saints' and 'New Testament saints' although the Bible has something to say about the distinctions there too.   Instead, I will orient my comments toward those who are believers today (although the same applies for all who believed in Jesus Christ since the time of His death and resurrection, but are 'asleep' as Paul terms it).   Here is how I distinguish these four phases:

1. After we die, we are ushered into another dimension Jesus called *Paradise*. Summing up this state (from considerable research I've done through the years), it appears we will recognize and encounter others. Our experience there is to be vibrant and wonderful, substantive *but not physical*. We will be conscious, but our perception will be quite different than how we experience reality today. Descriptions are consistent about hearing singing, seeing beautiful sites, talking with loved ones, and feeling that the experience is superlative to our best times on earth. We will communicate. But we will not be 'physical creatures.' This step into eternity is frequently the subject of books and movies. Testimonies abound of the dying departing with smiles on their faces from what they perceive 'in their mind's eye' just in front of them. Whether or not we traverse a dark tunnel and see a light at the end as many secular stories depict, isn't crystal clear. But what Paul teaches is *"to be absent from the body is to be present with the Lord."* (II Corinthians 5:8) Paul relates we won't experience a moment of loneliness or a sense of separation from God. If we believe in Jesus Christ and the Holy Spirit dwells in us, the Spirit of Christ is with us from the first moment our body turns off the switches until we are resident in God's reassuring presence. It isn't angels escorting us into the presence of God. It is the Spirit of Christ Himself.

2. Stage two is subject to much debate among Bible-believing Christians. This experience commences at the time of Jesus Christ's physical return to the earth when His bride (the 'Church') is 'raptured' to join Christ in the air. At that moment, our experience once again becomes physical despite being 'in the clouds.' Somehow, if we've experienced death, we'll be transported from 'Paradise' back to the upper atmosphere of the earth. Our physical body is resurrected and is rejoined with our spirit / soul. Our physical body is changed. Now, this is where the debate is joined. Either we will continue on from our presence in the clouds to return to the surface of the earth (which is the so-called post-

tribulation rapture view), or we will once again return to where we were previously, the 'other dimensional reality' (as the 'pre-tribulation rapture' doctrine asserts). We will have physical bodies once more, but our surroundings will continue to be in 'Paradise.' According to most evangelicals (within the so-called *Dispensational* view), we will likely remain in this state for at least seven more years (according to how time is kept upon the earth), until Jesus returns at the Battle of Armageddon to defeat Antichrist and his armies. We will be physical creatures but reside in a realm distinct from what we now call 'space-time.' Paul tells us, *"Then we which are alive [and] remain shall be caught up together with them in the clouds, to meet the Lord in the air: and so shall we ever be with the Lord."* (I Thessalonians 4:17) Some may object that this is illogical; the two realms can't be traversed in this way. To that objection, I point out Jesus Christ was resurrected and possessed a physical body that could be touched. He could eat and drink. He urged his followers to see *He was not a ghost.* (See John's gospel, chapters 20, 21) He was a physical being. And yet, when he ascended into Heaven, He ascended into a cloud with His physical body intact. This is the precedent for the 'stage two' *life after death* the Bible promises.

3. Then there is stage three. As in a novel, this is the 'climax.' For those who believe in the Bible and profess the Second Coming of Christ happens in 'space-time,' we return with Jesus at the Battle of Armageddon. We are His Saints. We are the 'clouds of heaven.' There are so many of us, dressed all in white (thanks to His redeeming death cleansing us from all our sin), to those mortals on earth we appear like clouds rolling in at the seashore. We will be a portentous sight. From this moment forward our experience returns to 'space-time' and we live physically upon the earth. The Bible is quite explicit in both the Old and New Testaments: We will

reside on this earth.[†] The Kingdom of the Messiah is the Kingdom of Jesus Christ. John tells us that His Kingdom will last for 1,000 years. However, that is not the end of things.

4. Finally, there is to be a New Heaven and a New Jerusalem that follows after this 1,000-year period. This is the dénouement. Just like a novel, it's the final stage when all questions are answered and everything becomes exceedingly clear. With the race won, the ultimate prize is awarded. John describes this as "a new world coming." Peter reveals God purges the entire universe of a persistent flaw which even throughout the Millennium is not fully corrected. John describes the New Jerusalem with breathtaking language suggesting the "streets are paved with gold" and all structures composed of a precious metal or some manner of jewel. Paul exclaims the entire creation yearns for this moment. *"But as it is written, 'Eye hath not seen, nor ear heard, neither have entered into the heart of man, the things which God hath prepared for them that love him.'"* (I Corinthians 2:9, quoting Isaiah 64:4) In this moment, suddenly time and space are reconfigured in an unimaginable way. Heaven and earth unite; time and eternity conjoin. The sun and moon are no longer needed for light. The Glory of God persists and provides unending light. We can't fully fathom this experience. What we can gather: Our participation in this reality will extend beyond our wildest dreams.

In thinking about my father's ideas about heaven, one fault I do find: It's 'short-sighted' it doesn't look far enough into the future. We should realize despite how wonderful the world will be when there is no longer political strife, natural

---

[†] G.H. Pember poses a slightly nuanced view of this 'endgame.' He speculates that the purpose of the Saints is to replace the 'spirits' under the direction of Satan, "The Prince and Power of the Air." Our authority will extend from earth to 'the 2nd heaven' – managing the world from a 'birds-eye view' of what's happening on the world.

disasters, or personal tragedies – when sickness is forgotten and when death is done away – 'the best is still yet to be.' An earth made like heaven is a great story. But there is much more about the afterlife to contemplate. As I said earlier, it's more like celebrating 12 days of Christmas rather than only one. Each stage of 'what comes next' builds upon the previous. We will soon learn that there is no such thing as 'as good as it gets.' An infinite God has the ability to enhance continually the spectacular. My concept of heaven and earth may be more complex than my father's, but I venture it holds much more promise.

So in the years ahead, if you hear me talk or write about my ideas about heaven and earth, one thing I do hope you will do for me: Allow me to repeat myself. For I find the prospects too awesome to be the subject of only one or two conversations, sermons, or books.

FOR FURTHER THOUGHT: Does your concept of the afterlife, frighten you, bore you, or excite you? Is heaven really just 'pie in the sky by and by' or is it a motivation for living a consecrated lifestyle today? Do you find it too hard to imagine the afterlife such that is has little value for your life today? Do you find the prospects of the earth being refreshed and renewed (whereupon it becomes a dwelling place for 1,000 years) too fantastic to believe? Do you feel it's a proper interpretation of what John teaches in the Book of Revelation? Do you believe the streets of the new Heaven will be paved with gold? Do you wonder if eternity could become boring?

9: Doom and Gloom

*And there shall be signs in the sun, and in the moon, and in the stars; and upon the earth distress of nations, with perplexity; the sea and the waves roaring; **Men's hearts failing them for fear, and for looking after those things which are coming on the earth**: for the powers of heaven shall be shaken. And then shall they see the Son of man coming in a cloud with power and great glory. And when these things begin to come to pass, then look up, and lift up your heads; for your redemption draweth nigh.*
(Luke 21:25-28)

THERE'S A COMMON SAYING, "YOU HAVE TO TAKE THE BAD WITH THE GOOD." APPARENTLY, IT'S STANDARD OPERAT- ING PROCEDURE FOR US COMMON FOLK: WHEN GOOD things happen, bad things come right alongside too. We natu- rally believe it's impossible for everything to go perfect. The wisdom of life seems to predict that bad and good are coupled. You can't have one without the other. Like Frank Sinatra's classic song preaches, *"Love and marriage, go together like a horse and carriage... Dad was told by my mother, you can't have one without the other, love and marriage go together."* Not that I'm saying *love* is good and *marriage* is bad... alt- hough maybe that was the not-so-hidden message in the song! Mamma had to remind Daddy, "Hey, there is no free lunch! You want my love? Get on your knee and propose to me!"

If we think about it more deeply, I suppose we could get philo- sophical and assert that we can only experience the good if we know what it's like to experience the bad. Our knowledge of either depends upon comparing the two. We need contrast to distinguish one from the other. A cold glass of water tastes a lot better when we are 'dying of thirst' than it does when we are in 'fluid balance' as my wife the nurse says. When it comes to 'getting in shape,' the adage exhorts us to recall that 'without pain there is no gain.' Or we can recall that famous recipe for a summer beverage: "Take the lemons life gives you and make lemonade." And finally there is that other conventional wisdom, "You can't make an omelet without breaking some eggs."

I've sometimes experienced periods during my life when if I'd have a good day, it would be automatic the next day would be bad – or at least *not as good.* Consequently, after I'd conclude, "Wow, today was a great day" then I'd remind myself, "Beware: The next day will be a lot less happy." Time after time, this experience played itself out. Perhaps it was the failure on my part to be positive and optimistic. Indeed, maybe the bad that followed the good was something of a self-fulfilling prophecy. Those who promote the 'power of positive thinking' would certainly fault me along those lines. You get what you expect. It's hard to argue that point. It's often true.

In my defense, my *peculiar* outlook is actually pretty typical. It comes from a universal, deep-seated superstition built upon this same recognition: "Don't be too enthusiastic about your success today – don't say anything out loud about it. The 'spirits will hear you and spoil your fun.'" We golfers joke about 'the golf gods' that *get even with us* when we brag too much about how great a shot we just made. Sure enough, a great shot is more often than not followed by a *laugher* (not that we find it easy to laugh when this happens!) Even the old superstition about 'knocking on wood' (after a positive affirmation) links to this idea: Rapping on wood awakens the spirits living inside the wood. These spirits promise protection from fates who seek retaliation (i.e., 'smacking us down' as my kids might say) for such boisterous confidence.

One of the most common reactions amongst those of us who are excited about biblical prophecy is for someone around us, typically someone we love, to chide us for being full of *doom and gloom.* We might be asked, "How can you sleep at night believing what you do about the end of the world?" Perhaps in self-defense I've come to jokingly call myself, "Doomsday Doug" since I'm now a published author on the topic of Bible prophecy. It's as if I expect a frontal assault in reaction to my public stance. By calling myself a name and going 'not okay' (as they teach in the practical psychology known as transactional analysis, or 'TA'), I defuse the anticipated missile soon to be launched my way.

But it's hard to escape the reality of what the Bible teaches. The redemption we pursue arrives at the height of world-wide calamity. 'Going to heaven' comes at the time when the world is literally 'going to hell.' Our joy arises simultaneous with the terror of those around us who don't share the same hope. Jesus predicted that in our times (paraphrasing), "Men's hearts shall fail them for fear of what they see coming to pass in the world." If we willingly admit to those around us we believe in Bible prophecy and expect to witness terrible signs in our lifetime, we know we're destined to 'hear about it.' It seems getting 'raked over the coals' by those who don't share our enthusiasm – being a proponent for *doom and gloom* – just goes with the territory.

To be sure, most of the experts in Bible prophecy agree: Fearful signs in the heavens, massive earthquakes, terrible storms, plagues, and catastrophes one right after another accompany the time of Jesus' return. If a particular cataclysm appears especially heinous, we often hear the descriptive phrase used, "it's of biblical proportions." The populace may know little about Bible prophecy. However, everyone knows that if a cataclysmic transpires, many conclude Bible's prophecies about the end times are coming true. Even the biblically illiterate recall the freakish judgments of the Bible: Water turning to blood, locus attacks, the sun growing dark, and stars falling from the heavens. Yes, even the unbelievers remember the 'bad' in the Bible. We can certainly thank lots of apocalyptic movies and TV shows for this little bit of Bible education amongst the masses.

In January of 2011, just after New Year's Day, we heard portentous reports worldwide regarding thousands of birds falling dead from the sky. News anchors could hardly contain themselves. They quickly labeled it, the "A-*flock*-alypse." They intimated we could laugh about it, even if it was no laughing matter. This not-so-funny quip suggested this strange event might be an omen of the world's end. Of course, immediately after spouting their well-turned phrase, our news people reassured us the situation is under control. They reported several noteworthy naturalists had clarified these 'die offs' happen all the time. There's no need to worry.

Well, perhaps that's true. Then again, perhaps there's something apocalyptic concerning these puzzling deaths. Could this be the start of a pole reversal where the North and South Pole flip? We know that animals navigate by sensing the 'lines' in the planet's magnetic field. We could logically assume that if our magnetic field is so radically altered, nature won't teach animals rapidly how to adjust to this change. Predictably (and sadly), millions of animals could die. We know Science believes our poles could flip at any time and that we are 'past due' for this to happen.* When this pole reversal occurs, our magnetic field virtually dissolves until the polarity completely reverses, whereupon Nature reinstates it. Many of the 2012 doomsayers believe this event will occur at the same

---

* This flipping is recorded in the composition of rocky material at the bottom of the ocean. Fault lines where the 'spreading' originates on the ocean's floor, serves as a magnetic recorder of the direction of the polarity of the earth at certain times in the past. We know these 'flips' occur every 100,000 to 200,000 years. The Sun also reverses its polarity in 11 year cycles, coinciding with sunspot activity. When these two cycles coincide as they are predicted by some to do in 2012, we would experience a cataclysm 'of biblical proportions.'

moment when the Sun's sunspot activity peaks. The Sun will spew higher levels of radioactivity our way at just the same time our planet's *shields are down* (to borrow a phrase from *Star Trek*). The result: We could experience power blackouts, radiation burns, and massive die offs of animals of all sorts, including *Homo sapiens*. Does the Bible confirm this will happen? No, but science reasons it's a plausible scenario.

If you study the Bible from cover to cover, the plain meaning of Scripture is 'the day of reckoning is coming.' *The Day of the Lord* is spoken of by all the prophets of the Old Testament; and in the New Testament, of course, it's renamed, *The Day of Jesus Christ*. This time will be an unmitigated season of colossal judgment. The Scripture confirms this scenario again and again. If we believe the Bible, even if we don't like to think about such horrible possibilities, we must affirm *it's undeniably a frequent subject*.

Without question, the cataclysms described in the prophecies of both the Old and New Testaments frighten us. We're told the experience of these 'last days' results from God's wrath directed at an unbelieving world. The Book of Revelation delves into details using remarkable symbols of judgment. There are *Seven Seals, Seven Trumpets,* and *Seven Bowls of Wrath:* Each breaking seal discloses a new horror; each trumpet portends a new calamity greater than the previous; each vial of wrath pours forth judgments whose description grows increasingly more horrible. If we dwell on these images of doom, no doubt we would become gloomy. Nevertheless, the Bible consistently offers a starkly contrasted message: The greatest day for those who believe in Christ, comes on the worst day for those that don't.

However, the Bible instructs Christians not to focus on this message of doom and gloom. We must *"lift up our heads for our redemption is at hand."* We should choose to accentuate the positive! We shouldn't dwell on the horrors soon to happen. We should set our minds on the good things just ahead.

The story of Lot and his family fleeing the judgment of Sodom and Gomorrah holds a lesson for us today. Most everyone (once again, even the biblically illiterate) knows of Sodom and Gomorrah. This city was so evil God determined to destroy it in a manner unlike any other judgment mentioned in the Bible. Archeologists studying this area in the Holy Lands consider the possibility Sodom and Gomorrah was destroyed by an atomic explosion: 'Fire and brimstone' literally rained down from the heavens. Could God have 'nuked' the city? Ancient alien astronaut theorists are certain this happened. While I may not agree with their depiction of God (who they believe to be an extraterrestrial intelligence), intriguingly the non-orthodox corroborate an exceptional source destroyed this area of the Middle East 4,000 years ago through some matchless method.

In the biblical account, we learn a problem existed in God's plan to judge these two cities on the plains of Israel. God had 'His people' in the city of Sodom: *Lot, the brother of Abraham* lived there. Furthermore, Lot had two daughters and a wife. The book of II Peter (2:7) tells us Lot was a righteous man tormented by the sin of this contemptuous city surrounding him. Consequently, like a special team of commandos, God prepared to perform an extraction of the righteous before the unrighteous of Sodom and Gomorrah could be destroyed.

Genesis 18 and 19 tells us God sent three special agents (His angels) to carry out this plan of judgment. But first the three angels traveled to see Abraham and Sarah (his wife) in order to give Abraham a 'heads up' that they were on their way to destroy these cities; whereupon Abraham began negotiating with the angel-in-charge (who many scholars believe was the pre-existent Christ and whom the Bible identifies as "the LORD"). Abraham questioned the first angel about how many righteous persons had to be in the city before God would forsake His plan (unquestionably, Abraham sensed that the 'lead' angel was much more than a mere angel).

This negotiation took place because Abraham misunderstood God's plan and more importantly, because he misunderstood *the nature of God.* It's quite clear God didn't intend to destroy the city with the 'good guys' still living there. First, God would rescue the righteous, extract them, and then judge Sodom and Gomorrah. In this discourse, God sought to express to Abraham that while judgment was coming He would protect Abraham's brother and his family. If Abraham had thought about it further, perhaps he would have realized, "Why else would God come see me first?" However, God was teaching Abraham a lesson: *God rescues His people before He sends judgment.* Unlike the gods of Sumeria that Abraham grew up learning about as a child, Abraham's God was a *just* God – free of any taint of capriciousness. God didn't need Abraham or anyone else to tell Him 'how to do the right thing.'

Nevertheless, having not yet learned this lesson, Abraham negotiated with the LORD. He bargained with God and made the LORD agree He would drop His plan of judgment on behalf of no more than a mere *ten* righteous persons who might live in Sodom and Gomorrah (a number no doubt that Abraham calculated would include Lot's family, son-in-laws, and possible children Abraham supposed might be present).

In the account, two of the angels press ahead to Sodom while Abraham and the LORD finish their negotiation. When the two angels arrive at Sodom, Lot greets them, bows down before them (recognizing their other-worldly nature), and then brings the angels into his house where they spend the night – but not without incident. The Sodomites (all men, both young and old) bang on Lot's door and demand these guests be given to them to exploit sexually. Lot goes out to bargain with them and even offers his two virgin daughters to the crowd instead (apparently his daughters were betrothed to his son-in-laws but not married). But the angels refused to stand by and let Lot go through with his offer. They come to the door, pull Lot back into the house, and smite the crowd with blindness. Early the next morning (before the town was awake), the two angels gather Lot, his wife, and his two daughters together in order to flee the city (without the son-in-laws who mocked Lot when he asked them to join the escape party). The angels warned their little group of 'rescuees' to look forward and not backwards as they fled. The Scripture hints the party travels from the plains into the mountains, an appreciable distance. Later we learn Lot's wife apparently hears the thunder of judgment and senses the city's destruction. She turns to look from far away and instantly, turns into a pillar of salt having disregarded the angel's warning.[†] Evidently, Lot's wife couldn't fix her eyes on the good to come – she was still stuck in the mire of what lay behind.

The Bible says this event could be seen from many miles distant: *"And Abraham gat up early in the morning to the place where he stood before the LORD (negotiating): And he looked toward Sodom and Gomorrah, and toward all the land of the plain, and beheld, and, lo, the smoke of the country went up as the smoke of a furnace."* (Genesis 19:27-28) Did it resemble the ominous mushroom cloud of an atomic explosion? Abraham surely wondered whether Lot and his family were 'free and clear' of this destruction. If God hadn't warned Abraham, we can imagine Abraham would have headed right toward Sodom to learn of his brother's fate. Hence, we can see why God made

---

[†] Many have speculated why Lot's wife received this peculiar judgment. The speculation is that she was unwilling to depart from the city. She didn't want to leave her life 'in the city' behind, perhaps proving her unworthiness to be saved. Her turning around was a willful decision and not an accidental glance. It probably wasn't the first 'about turn' she had done that day.

sure Abraham knew what was to happen. We're told the next action of Abraham is to 'head south' – no doubt to put more distance between his family and the awesome destruction he had witnessed. Were radiation involved, the story makes even more sense. God wouldn't have wanted the father of many nations walking amidst a ground covered in such poisoning. This would have put a real kink in God's greater plan – not to mention generating many mutations in the progenitor's DNA.

The Bible provides many lessons on how God moves to protect His people before His brings judgment on the unrighteous. We see this with Noah and his family, protected in the Ark while the world is judged with a massive flood. We will discuss in another essay how this reinforces the notion of the Rapture of the Church *before* judgment dawns upon the unbelieving world. But for now, the point is this: *Rejoice in God's upcoming salvation, even though His judgment comes too.* Praise Him for protecting and yes, *rescuing us from the terrors of the wrath to come.* We do have to take the bad with the good. It's sad the world is heading toward a horrible climax as the 'signs of the times' continue to mount. But we are to *"lift up our heads for our redemption draweth nigh."* Despite the impending doom, we are to rejoice that the good comes right alongside. The two must happen together.

So how should we respond to those who label us the 'doom and gloomers?' Perhaps we must remind them the Bible teaches we all have a choice. We rejoice in His provision to pull us out before doom strikes. We express sorrow so many choose not to embrace the opportunity to be *extracted*. Like Lot's son-in-laws who ignored the warnings of angels, unbelievers mock believers who hope to see these 'mockers' rescued. But at day's end, those who mock remain responsible for the choices they make. If they castigate us (however seriously or not-so-seriously) for bringing up the subject of the end times with the implicit allusion to the doom and gloom which lies ahead, we should be quick to point out it's not that we focus on doom and gloom, *it's just our redemption, that which we seek, happens at the same time.* Perhaps the Apostle Peter said it best when he reminded us that the apocalypse remains a future event because God's 'extraction program' is an ongoing activity (the 'snatch and grab' mission as they say in the military). He intends to pull to safety as many as He can. *"The Lord is not slack concerning his promise, as some men count slackness; but is longsuffering to us-ward, not willing that **any should perish**, but that all should come to repentance."* (II Peter 3:9)

Mama said, "We have to take the bad with the good." But God's offer looks beyond the destruction to the redemption and opportunity that lies on the other side. He reminds us our decisions have consequences. However, *His offer beckons us to choose life now.* After 40 years wondering in the wilderness, Moses exhorted the Children of Israel at the moment when they reached the cusp of their new life, as they stood ready to cross the Jordan, and enter into the Promised Land: *"I call heaven and earth to record this day against you, [that] I have set before you life and death, blessing and cursing: therefore choose life, that both thou and thy seed may live"* (Deuteronomy 30:19). The choices are clear: Blessing or cursing, life or death. Which will it be?

FOR FURTHER THOUGHT: Do we live each day hopeful that good will happen? Are we looking forward optimistically? Or are we like Lot's wife, bemoaning what we've lost in the past? When we do an 'about face,' what finally causes us to stop and turn around again heading in the right direction? What will it take for members of our family who scoff at the 'end-times scenario' to finally accept the Bible's testimony of what is to come? (Remember: Lot's son-in-laws saw angels 'smite' the Sodomites into blindness but still didn't believe judgment was coming).

10: Finding Meaning in Doomsday*

And as it was in the days of Noe (Noah), so shall it be also in the days of the Son of man. They did eat, they drank, they married wives, they were given in marriage, until the day that Noah entered into the ark, and the flood came, and destroyed them all. Likewise also as it was in the days of Lot; they did eat, they drank, they bought, they sold, they planted, they builded [built]; but the same day that Lot went out of Sodom it rained fire and brimstone from heaven, and destroyed them all. Even thus shall it be in the day when the Son of man is revealed.
(Luke 17:26-30)

I T'S NOT THAT UNCOMMON TO HEAR SOMEONE SAY, "THAT WHICH DOESN'T KILL US, ONLY MAKES US STRONGER." THE PHRASE IS ACTUALLY A POPULAR, ALBEIT SOMEWHAT CORrupted adaptation of a statement of Friedrich Nietzsche: "That which doesn't destroy us, defines us." There is considerable truth in this notion. I might personalize the wording even further: *Any challenge we overcome provides a compelling disclosure of who we really are.*

But in an unexpected way, those limits we can't overcome – especially the ultimate ones – also define who we are. Limitations, once accepted and embraced, can reveal *character* and what course our lives should take. This is what the philosopher Martin Heidegger taught. For him, death was the ultimate issue. Once we understand it's *the* inescapable reality, *paradoxically*, we may experience real meaning. But by denying death, we delay discovering the limited capacity we have to plot our course in this life and consequently, what our life is to mean.

In 1973, an important book was published that crossed the lines of philosophy, anthropology, and psychology. Written by

---

* This chapter is adapted and expanded from a portion of the concluding chapter of my book, *Decoding Doomsday*.

Ernst Becker, it was entitled, *The Denial of Death*. It won the Pulitzer Prize for non-fiction in 1974.

Becker asserts that, when it comes to the subject of our mortality, *human beings are double-minded*. On the one hand, we know we will die. On the other, we seem called to do something with our lives that is heroic, which proves our meaning. We seek a positive legacy. In short, *we strive to amount to something*. Becker says, "The hope and belief is that the things that man creates in society are of lasting worth and meaning, that they outlive or outshine death and decay, that man and his products count."[†]

The nightmare scenario: *Death* is both certain and permanent while *significance* is not only fleeting, it's ultimately fictional. Our lives are full of attempts to deny death. We build our character and identity upon our 'claim to fame.' We try to attach our worth to something we do or 'someone' we believe we are. This endeavor typically consumes us.

Becker believed that this effort was a necessary exercise for human beings to live in the world. However, this 'immortality project' (as he called it) prevents self-knowledge. We live in denial, hiding in dark shadows throughout our days, avoiding any light of awareness that might uncover the truth we are nothing more than finite beings with an unpredictable destiny. As Shakespeare laments in Macbeth's soliloquy:

> *Tomorrow and tomorrow and tomorrow,*
> *Creeps in this petty pace from day to day*
> *To the last syllable of recorded time,*
> *And all our yesterdays have lighted fools*
> *The way to dusty death. Out, out, brief candle!*
> *Life's but a walking shadow, a poor player*

[†] For additional information on Ernst Becker, please see *www.ernest-becker.com/thedenialofdeath*. Quote taken from the following page: *www.ernest-becker.com/ernest-becker-quotes*.

> *That struts and frets his hour upon the stage*
> *And then is heard no more: it is a tale*
> *Told by an idiot, full of sound and fury,*
> *Signifying nothing.*

In short, whether it's conscious or not, we persist in our self-deception. We ignore the Socratic admonition, "The unexamined life is not worth living." We disregard the hard truth about what makes us tick. We may fool others – but we surely fool ourselves.

Becker presses the point that *evil* is what happens when we *deny our mortality and seek to destroy all threats to what we deem our source for meaning.* Religious wars would certainly fall into this category, but so would the efforts to overturn religion in the name of science.

While Becker may be guilty of dramatizing *the evil that men do* being so heavily influenced as he was by the holocaust, it's inadequate to offer a summary characterization of his views with no more than a clichéd phrase like *human behavior is self-ish and self-seeking.* Indeed, his insight into our underlying motivation is a genuine breakthrough: We do evil primarily to protect our *immortality project,* our claim to fame. If someone dares to upset what we perceive substantiates our self-worth, we are quick to strike out against any and all such perpetrators. We feel compelled to eliminate such threats because we preserve the basis for life's meaning – it's sacred – there's nothing more important to us whether we are conscious of it or not.

While Becker didn't use these exact words, nonetheless they concisely state his position: Our *quest to protect life's meaning becomes the root of our evil.* Let's administer a self-test:

- What is your most 'cherished' belief giving meaning to your life?

- *What happens when someone challenges this belief?* Are you angry or threatened? Are you quick to strike back?

- *What is the reason for your belief?* Is the foundation of your faith immune to any sort of *proof to the contrary*?

If we're being honest, any contradiction posed to our most treasured belief, if unexamined, is a *flash point*. We won't let the matter go and walk away. We will strike back – no holds barred – to reassure ourselves we *still have it right*. My point being: It's dangerous to ask ourselves why we believe what we do; but it's even more dangerous *not* to face the possibility our beliefs could be dead wrong.

In light of these insights which mirror so much wisdom from many other religions and philosophers through the ages, what should we to make of the phenomenon we call *doomsday*?

If we're like most people, we avoid thinking about it. At some point, however, we may conclude, it's a topic we can't evade. After all, there's now so much discussion about the threats of war, disease, planetary catastrophe, and wild weather – the apprehension grows daily. *Doomsday is impossible to ignore.*

Confronted as we are with the realistic possibility of *doomsday,* how should we react? Certainly, we must feel endangered. However, isn't this fear easily dismissed? Isn't doomsday just like *the denial of death,* but on a 'whole-species' basis? After all, is there anything more shattering to our notion of meaning, if something – no matter how straightforward or sinister – was to wipe our entire species off the face of the planet?

It quickly becomes apparent our notion of God (is He or isn't He real?) has a lot to do with how we handle our predicament. For those who believe in an infinite creator God, a personal being who broods over his creation, that (as evangelical Christians preach) desires a 'personal relationship with us,' how could we possibly believe God would allow such a thing? Certainly, we base our *shared sense of meaning* upon an overt notion our existence on this planet is no accident. Something or someone greater created us – there is no way that God would allow all of life to expire. Surely, He would even overturn our free will if we were hell-bent on destroying the planet (and ourselves). For those of us who believe in the reality of a divine presence in the universe (however we understand *the divine being*), there is little doubt about our conclusion: *Evil won't prevail.* The good guys come out on top.

On the other hand, if we believe there is no God, perhaps we might sooner come to grips with at least the theoretical possibility that a future cataclysm will end civilization and the entire human species. With the absence of *God as a protector*, there's no longer any insurance against annihilation – there's no guardian upon which we can rely – there's no higher-power left to watch over us. We are *left to our own devices*.

Some would state stoically, "The sooner we accept this bleak truth, the better off we are." Indeed, many would counsel this is a much more honest way to approach the matter of doomsday. After all, isn't counting on God's intervention on our behalf – preventing us from destroying ourselves – dishonest, negligent, and even reprehensible? Doesn't atheism, in this context, demand we take responsibility for our actions far more than relying upon God?

For the moment, let's say this is so. The question then arises, "When it comes to whether we should dismiss all meaning to our existence, is the atheist capable of being consistent with his or her own presuppositions?" Can he or she actually get comfortable with the starkness of a universe without God? We ask this question because we know that, despite what we say we believe, at the end of the day we are all very much alike. The quest for meaning is part of our DNA just as much as our denial of death; in fact, it's one and the same.

Just consider how the *unbeliever* acts when tragedy occurs. He might cry out, 'Why me?' like anyone else; when he should remember such questions imply faith in life's purpose – which his stated belief system expressly denies. How can there be *misfortune* if we begin with no guarantees and no destiny? If there is no God to offer explanations, how can we obtain answers? If there are no fates to cause the occurrence, how can we look for a reason to explain it?

When bad things happen to good people, the last person that should be shocked is the atheist. The atheist truly can't label any catastrophe *a tragedy*. It is what it is. The cry goes out to the stars and the sky, but the universe answers with silence.

That's why atheism is so inconsistent with humanity's wiring. When calamity strikes, *even the most pessimistic atheist is stunned*. The unbeliever, just like the believer, expects better. The atheist too feels the same initial *sense that there must still be hope*. Accordingly, we shouldn't wonder why the atheist, just like a person of faith, gets upset if something bad happens. The reality is *even the atheist loses his or her equanimity* when an outcome seems brutal or unjust. In our better moments, we all anticipate social justice and positive outcomes. It may only be instinctual in the human 'animal.' But we believe somewhere there *is a guarantor for the good*.

That's why, even for the atheistic materialist, an indisputable aspect of human expectation insists *there is something beyond ourselves*. The reality of this underlying conviction defies even the hard-core atheist to mutter 'so what' at our demise. Our optimism, our *assurance* (which often needs to be *re-assured* by our loved ones, a good book, or an uplifting sermon) remains a part of humanity's essence. Therefore, we build our love and aspirations upon a rock called *meaning*. What happens *does matter*, not just to us, but to *the grand scheme of things*. We want to believe every person deserves a happy ending. It's my belief we all share this confidence in life's meaning because God planted this in our being. It's *an innate testimony to God's existence* since it inspires our best moments and causes us to seek justice, love, and ultimately Him. I won't suggest this recognition provides 'proof' of God's existence. This 'theorem' isn't up there with Thomas Aquinas' 'unmoved mover' or other cosmological arguments, but it's a standard human attribute implying God left His thumbprint on our 'inner person.'

Perhaps paradoxically, and very much on the other hand, I insist we meditate on the possibility *of a universe without God*. Even the faithful should thoughtfully consider this perspective despite giving appearance to a moment of infidelity.

From this vantage point, the search for *meaning* could indeed be nothing more than a primal delusion to which we all succumb – a survival mechanism we must outgrow. We may all share in a happy but false fantasy about what life means. Perhaps it's nothing more than *a diabolical curse* because every day we uncritically quest after fairness and significance. If it's indeed no more than a diabolical trick, then our best and most noble ambitions are destined to fail.

While our optimism may be nothing more than a deception making life bearable, Becker (and others who consider themselves existentialists), nevertheless insist we squarely face this possibility, however theoretical. The *absurd* could be our lot. Before we search for a way out of this metaphorical dungeon, we should recognize we might not find a doorway. We must consider the distinct possibility we can't rid ourselves of the chains of meaninglessness.

As a teenager, I remember a popular expression cast about by many to help keep things in perspective: *Today is the first day of the rest of your life*. This notion was a refreshing way of recognizing we can put our past behind us and start anew. Yet, the abrupt converse of this statement may be better medicine awakening us to our 'existential situation:' *Today could be the last day of our life*.

For believers and unbelievers alike, we don't awaken in the mornings with this thought firmly in mind as we live out each day. If we did, we probably wouldn't get out of bed! However, it doesn't make the possibility any less stark. The fact remains: A bus might run over us today or tonight an asteroid could decimate our planet. Either way, our mortal life ends. Our consciousness comes to a halt. Perhaps we can avoid the former by staying at home. However, the latter possibility is one we can literally do nothing to circumvent.

So how should we deal with such fear? How do we *put dooms-day into perspective?*

When they are young, we read fairy tales to our children. But the tales we read today are highly sanitized versions of the old *Grimm's Fairy Tales* (first published in 1810). What we may not realize is just how grim these fairy tales were. The monsters and witches were much darker then, heroes were much more vulnerable, and the deaths of the villains much more gruesome.

Why did our forebears tell such frightful stories to their children? We know now it was how parents prepared their children for the reality of the dark world in which they lived. Evil was commonplace. Better to scare them to death early exposing them to the horrors of life, for such things were to be their firsthand experience sooner rather than later. It was in the parent's best judgment this sort of *tough love* was necessary conditioning as part of growing up.

This perspective contrasts so much with our protective methods of child rearing today, perhaps we should ask ourselves, "Which generation was right?" Should we teach our children evil is easy to overcome, that death is easy to cheat? On the other hand, do we help our children understand that death is a part of life? Should they learn evil sometimes wins and disasters occur? What type of reassurance is the proper balance between hoping for the best and not being surprised if bad things happen? The prayer I used to say at bedtime (like many other baby boomers) included the line, "If I should die before I wake, I pray the Lord my soul to take." As a child, I didn't fear death. Nor did this prayer scare me to death either. Somehow knowing God was watching over me, even as I slept, was a comforting thought.

We sometimes employ the phrase *whistling in the dark* when we're afraid to face the dire circumstances in our way. What do we mean by this adage? What is the underlying motive for whistling a happy tune while we 'walk about' fearing what might come next?

In essence, our whistling *normalizes* the situation; it makes our circumstances less imposing. Sometimes psychiatrists will describe this phenomenon as *minimizing* whatever threat disrupts our normal course of life. You know the familiar phrase, "The bigger they are the harder they fall." We may not believe it. Nonetheless, by saying this phrase smartly, we muster the courage to face our enemies.

My family did this so very well it took me many years to learn how to deal with death and suffering. Our approach was to laugh it off or get things back to normal as quickly as we could. We might typically say something like "It's no big deal." We wouldn't face the possibility the worse could happen and that we might not be able to cope. Instead of learning to square up to bad times and face the music, it was our habit to escape the pain. This failure to come to terms with tragedy and suffering almost ended my marriage 27 years ago when my father-in-law died from Lou Gehrig's disease (ALS) and I couldn't relate to my wife's feelings as she watched her father's health disintegrate before her eyes.

My supposition is we have two essential methods of dealing with death from doomsday – one healthy, the other, *not so much*. These are deep-seated human techniques to cope with drastic situations. The two phenomena outlined above give us a glimpse of what these methods are.

Method One: *Recognize that the cataclysm not only can happen, but it's eventually inevitable*. Furthermore, our encounter may be immediately ahead. We may embrace it and calculate how we should live our lives in its light. We may make our meaning no longer contingent upon the denial of mortality and our particular and cherished plan for self-worth. We may recognize we are finite beings who trusts our value secured *only after* it's linked to something much bigger than us. In the case of those in the Judeo-Christian tradition, we may connect who we are and what our life means *to God*, whose infinite status assures our value. He is our point of reference. In other words, *we have meaning because God tells us we mean something to Him*. Moreover, the proof is in His promise – our lives are so valuable He will transform them – making them fit for eternity. As the evangelical intellectual Francis Schaeffer asserted: *Finite beings have meaning only if they have an infinite point of reference*.

Method Two: *Find ways to reduce the potential for doomsday*. Our culture, now more than ever, obsesses over *the end of days*. Doomsday captivates us. Our popular culture is chock-full of examples. So then, as a culture, do we *really* deny doomsday? It seems – at least on the surface – that nothing could be further from the truth. However, sometimes things aren't quite what they seem.

In our defense, we insist we are taking action. We seek to dispel the worry and the gloom of doom. We read books. We go to movies. However, our captivation is much more akin to *whistling in the dark* than assimilating frightening images medicinally *through the fairy tale*. We encounter the darkness to reassure ourselves it isn't a menacing presence after all. We vaccinate ourselves with just enough of what could happen to comfort ourselves that it won't. It simply is too fantastic – so out of the question – why would we lose any sleep over it?. We venture out to a movie and watch the world end in the best special effects ever. After all, it's *only a movie*. The sun will rise again tomorrow. Life will go on.

So, if you accept my conclusion, what does the doctor prescribe? Simply this: It's best to acknowledge the end can happen *at any moment*. We may realize our worst fears. We shouldn't deny it. We should embrace it. This doesn't mean we have to rejoice in it. But we best acknowledge its reality. Even if we cling, I believe rightly, to faith as our means to overcome anxiety and to resolve what may otherwise appear absurd, it's wise to recognize the dilemma in which we find ourselves. Once we appreciate our *existential* condition, we live a life that is far more authentic. Even from the perspective of the most pious and stalwart Christian, before any of us can fully appreciate *the salvation message*, we should fully understand *our predicament if we didn't have the gift of salvation.*

Who hasn't experienced a *narrow escape*, when someone you loved nearly 'bought the farm?' Perhaps it was a spouse. Perhaps it was a child. When we finally realize our loved one is okay, this resolution quiets our worst fears. Yet, we still never quite forget the feeling of *dread* we just experienced. Being grateful, we may be forever changed. Living in light of that experience reminds us to keep our eyes wide open, be a bit more cautious, and take extra pains to protect those we love. After this happens, if we fail to appreciate this impact, we've wasted what the calamity sought to teach us.

A wise person once said: "Pagans waste their pains" – which is a statement of concise conviction that something or someone greater than ourselves is teaching a lesson we must learn. Nietzsche scolded his readers for not recognizing *all progress comes through pain.* Seeking only pleasure as a cherished goal in life is a death knell for personal growth and meaning.

The 'conventionally wise' wonder why people like 'prophecy buffs' believe doomsday is no myth but is a historical inevitability. We can imagine those folk casting aspersions along the lines of: "Why are you so consumed with such bleak prognostications? Why don't you look on the bright side?"

Our response could be simply, "Because we have to face facts. And the fact is sooner or later, whether you listen to science or to the Bible, one manner of doomsday or another is inevitable." Like Becker and other existentialists who proposed that death is the inescapable destiny which awakens us to reality – teaching us how to live – doomsday is an unavoidable reality causing humanity to come to grips with our limits and what actions we must take *now*. Some disasters we can avoid altogether while others we can do little more than reduce their effects. But who disagrees with the admonition that it's better to be prepared than to live blithely as if nothing like doomsday could ever happen, even if it's only 'regional', i.e., in our neck of the woods?

Noah was a unique person. He was told by God that doomsday was coming. What's more, he was told specifically what he must do in order to assure his family (and all land creatures from lambs to lions!) would survive doomsday. We can imagine how believing in doomsday would cause his contemporaries to laugh him to scorn for such a crazy thought. How much more would they scoff at him for building a boat miles from an ocean? But he knew doomsday was inevitable; God had told him so. While everyone else continued on, living life as usual, eating and drinking (thinking short-term), marrying and giving in marriage (thinking long-term), Noah and his sons were preparing for the end of the world. Clearly, in a very unique way, doomsday gave Noah purpose and meaning!

Today, we know there are many types of regional and even global catastrophes science can prove have precedent. There are also warnings about future wars we read plainly in the Bible. Will we be like Noah who took extraordinary measures to be prepared or like his neighbors who gathered often just to jeer him? God may not be asking us to build an ark; nonetheless He is asking us to prepare ourselves and those we love for the inevitable.

Perhaps we should *adapt* the prayer of theologian Reinhold Niebuhr, made famous by Alcoholics Anonymous: *God grant us the serenity to preempt those catastrophes we can, prepare ourselves for the calamities we are helpless to deflect, and the wisdom to know the difference.*

FOR FURTHER THOUGHT: Do the plans we have for our lives and those we love reflect the reality that we are finite creatures who can't control everything that happens? What belief do we hold about who we are that supplies meaning to our lives? Can we identify what our immortality project is? Is it raising children? Is it how well we perform at our job? Is it writing a best-selling book? How do we react if we feel someone is treading on our 'immortality project?' What are we doing to prepare ourselves for the inevitable? Do we trust in God such that we realize whatever our existence means is ultimately because God directs us to achieve His purpose for our lives? Do we believe it is helpful to 'embrace' doomsday as described in this chapter?

11: Connecting Origins and Destiny

Knowing this first, that there shall come in the last days scoffers, walking after their own lusts, and saying, "Where is the promise of his coming? For since the fathers fell asleep, all things continue as they were from the beginning of the creation." For this they willingly are ignorant of, that by the word of God the heavens were of old, and the earth standing out of the water and in the water: Whereby the world that then was, being overflowed with water, perished.
(II Peter 3:3-6)

WHEREVER WE ARE ON THE ROAD OF OUR LIVES, WE MUST REALIZE THAT WE DIDN'T JUST APPEAR WHERE WE FIND OURSELVES WITHOUT TAKING A SERIES OF other highways to get us here. First we take one road. Then we take another. We make choices. Sometimes we're puzzled and ask ourselves, "How did I wind up here?" But memories serve as breadcrumbs lying in the paths taken, marking the trail we chose along the way. Another way to express this observation: Our lives are like steps on a vast stairway. Each day is a step. Where we are now is a result of the steps we have taken to arrive at our destination.

How we explain 'who we are' begins with where we started out. Who I am today is a result of a collection of people I've known, events I've experienced, lessons I've learned, and decisions I've made. It's a combination of what's happened to me and how I've reacted to those myriad events each and every day.

Surely whoever we are at this moment results from many such matters. Like stones placed on the exterior wall of a giant house, each stone is placed precisely one at a time. Unlike bricks, each stone is unique and has to fit exactly with all the others in a very specific way. Fitting the stones together takes creativity. It isn't easy to build a good looking house unless the stonework is performed by a master mason who knows exactly what he or she is doing.

The nutritionist says, "You are what you eat." The existentialist says, "You are what you do." A Christian says, "I am what God enables me to become."

For those who believe in the providence of God, without denying our personal responsibility, we believe that somehow God is that expert mason, placing the stones we call life events in just exactly the right spot, considering carefully the shape of every stone, so that once the house is complete it looks *smart*; it evinces a grand design. Undoubtedly, that's the way we want our lives to appear when the last stone of our life is put in place.

When I spoke at my mother's funeral a few years ago, I quoted a particular saying that she loved. It was a simple verse that I once used my gift of calligraphy to 'engross' upon parchment. The verse was, "What I am is God's gift to me; what I become is my gift to God." Being artistic and eager to make a few dollars for my work, I became quite adept at practicing the art of the medieval monks. When I was a teenager, folks knew me as an artist.

At the funeral, I talked about the influence of my mom, how she contributed to the person I then was. Despite my mom's idiosyncrasies (some of them not so charming), she loved her kids and cared for us as only a loving mother could (indeed, sometimes maybe too much!). At the service my point was, how we influence others is a 'gift that keeps on giving.' A life well-lived, lives on, continuing its influence in the world through the lives of those who continue the journey. It's a rather obvious tribute to the person eulogized. And yet, it's an awesome thought: We affect the world even after we're no longer here.

Afterwards, I realized I'd never felt prouder of anything I've ever said in a public forum. I still feel that way today. Perhaps someone will find something to say about me that affects them the same way at my funeral. I can only hope!

Decoding prophecy requires a paradoxical approach: To learn about our future we must study our past. Whether we search ancient sources of wisdom or study megalithic monuments holding hidden meanings, both archeology and written history hold the key to *eschatology*.* Our destiny is best understood after we uncover our origins. *We learn more about what our future holds, as our knowledge of the past grows.*

As we have discussed, Christians believe that prophetic studies are vital for many reasons. Part of this intensity stems from the knowledge that *the world in which we live will soon be rehabilitated.* This transformation will be massive and life-changing. This is especially so for those who anticipate this new world.

However, what I intend to discuss in this chapter will be astonishing to many readers because, on the surface, it doesn't appear to relate to how the world will be transformed *in the future*. My subject is quite the opposite. I venture readers will be astounded by what I share regarding how our world *was transformed in the past,* preparing for this *epoch of humankind.* The reason the topic is relevant relates to the verse from II Peter quoted as the epigraph for this chapter. The connection: To properly appreciate what will happen on the earth *after* Christ returns, we do well to comprehend what really happened to our world *before* Adam was created 'from the dust of the earth' by Elohim, the Creator.

The New Testament book of II Peter is one of the more controversial and questioned books by Bible critics who doubt its authenticity. My personal position: It contains some of the most intriguing and 'hidden' insights into the nature of the world, the cosmos, and what will happen in the millennium ahead. I believe to gain such insights the author must have experienced

---

* From *eschaton* in the Greek, meaning the study of 'last things.'

direct and special revelation by God. Following Christian con-
vention, such revelation was uniquely given to Christ's Apostles. Besides, since the book possesses a claim to be written by
Peter and the author testifies it's his second epistle, I go with
tradition and ascribe it to Peter. At the base of what many assume to be my gullibility is a principle I hold to be trustworthy:
It's difficult to assume there's credibility in a work written under a 'pen name' (i.e., a pseudonym).[†] Ultimate matters are
made more sure when the author isn't lying about who is responsible for the ideas contained within.

The passage cited above from II Peter makes little sense until
we understand that Peter is *disputing* the notion *that the
world today is the same as the world has always been.* Peter
is implying that what we see – the form of the world as we
observe it – is *not* because of the current and 'standard' processes we perceive. Dramatic, indeed radical events fashioned
the world in which we now live. Peter provides an amazing
analogy. Once we understand him, it becomes a powerful argument for rethinking why our world 'is in the shape that it's
in.' In short, it radically alters what we typically believe the
first Chapter of Genesis teaches. Additionally, it opens the
door to a completely different *cosmology* – including a proof
that future changes are all-the-more likely than what we
would have guessed *if* we didn't have these insights.

While it's quite common to doubt our world is subject to radical change in the future, Peter wants us to realize that the
'earth-bound' outlook is wrong: The truth regarding the na-

[†] Of course, higher criticism suggests all the books of the Bible, except
about half of Paul's letters, were not written by the authors as claimed
by tradition. In liberal theology, it's fashionable to allow fraudulent
claims, just because some ancient writers did this in order to impress
and influence their audiences to 'heed what the authors wrote.' Since
the liberal perspective believes spiritual truth is only 'views' it doesn't
really matter who spoke them.

ture of our earth, our solar system, and our universe is far different than what we suppose.

Peter's argument, reduced to its most basic form is rather simple: "Because the world has been dramatically transformed once before, it can and will be radically altered again in the future." Peter indicates that scoffers base their doubt of Christ's return from what they observe. They're empiricists – they believe all knowledge is gained through sense perception only.[‡] This stance supports their denial regarding what the Bible teaches about the world to come. Their repudiation of Christ's Second Coming begins with the wrongheaded opinion that the principles we see in operation today are exactly the same as they've been for millions of years gone by – and the way they will be for millions of years to come.

In geology, we call this the principle of 'uniformity.' This principle assumes the processes we witness today (slow and incremental), are the same processes that go back to 'time immemorial.' Peter argues how holding this view betrays a false understanding of the way the world was created. He teaches the world in which we live has gone through a dramatic re-creation and will go through another re-creation after Christ returns. This geologic principle is called 'catastrophism.' It's in stark contrast to the former. While generally mocked throughout the 20th century as a result of science's embrace of Darwinism (from the standpoint as a *theory of origins*), by referencing recent scientific discoveries[§] we now know there have been many enormous global cataclysms. From caldera eruptions to comet collisions, our world

---

[‡] In philosophy, this perspective is called *positivism*. As the world progresses toward spiritualism (an occult view), positivism is becoming passé. This is discussed in the classic, *The Morning of the Magicians* by Pauwels and Bergier.
[§] Most of these discoveries have occurred in the past two decades.

has experienced far more catastrophes than we once thought. Disasters have shaped our world and will continue to shape it in the future. Succinctly put: *What we witness as first-hand observers today does not tell us how we got to where we are now or where we are going next.* That is the essence of Peter's perspective. What is this insight really all about?

The stunning truth many classic Bible scholars teach us[**] is that the Bible doesn't really begin with 'today's creation' – the world as we know it – in Genesis 1:1. Yes, in the very beginning God made the heavens and the earth. However, the next verse assumes something happened after verse one and before verse two. Thus, the creation of the world as-we-know-it begins *in Genesis 1:2.*

What was this 'in-between' event? The whole of creation (or at least our solar system so some scholars suspect) became *chaos*. Unlike the gnostic and Greek notion, it didn't start that way. But something happened that caused things to go haywire. God's 'creation' in Genesis 1:2 was therefore a reordering of this chaos. It was literally, a 're-creation.'

Let's dig into this astounding notion further. The Bible, Moses, (and God as the real author) want us to recognize that God created the heavens and the earth (Genesis 1:1). But between Genesis 1:1 and Genesis 1:2 there was a gap of time in which violent things happened. Once we respect the entirety of Scripture's teaching, we discover this startling fact.

There is a good summary of this biblical cosmological theory, known as 'Gap Theory' in an article on Wikipedia. [††] I will paraphrase it here:

[**] Such scholars would include Clarence Larkin, J.N. Darby, and G.H. Pember and most 'dispensational' theologians of the 20th century.
[††] See *http://en.wikipedia.org/ wiki/Gap_Theory.*

- Space, time, water, and the rock which constitutes the main body of the earth, existed before the period of six days began in Genesis 1:3.

- God is perfect and everything He does is perfect, so a newly created earth from the hand of God shouldn't have been without form and void and shrouded in darkness. (See Deuteronomy 32:4, Isaiah 45:18 1 John 1:5)

- The Holy Spirit was "renewing" the face of the earth as He hovered over the face of the waters. (See Psalms 104:30)

- Angels already existed in a state of grace when God "laid the foundations of the Earth", so there had been at least one creative act of God before the six days of Genesis. (See Job 38:4-7)

- Satan had fallen from grace "in the beginning" which, since the serpent tempted Adam and Eve, had to have occurred before the 'fall' of humankind. (See Isaiah 14:12-15, Ezekiel 28:11-19, John 8:44).

Consequently, Genesis 1:2 has been mistranslated and therefore misunderstood. Traditionally, in the King James Version (and essentially most other versions echo the King James), it's translated "The earth was without form and void." But by taking it one-word-at-a-time and looking carefully at the Hebrew, the correct translation is much more likely to be "But the earth became chaotic and a wasteland."‡‡ Now, that's quite different. Something happened which caused the world to be corrupted and turned into a chaotic mess.

We don't know exactly what ensued. Most scholars who subscribe to this interpretation of Genesis believe the rebellion of Lucifer was the catalyst for the world to become such a wasteland. There are many unanswered questions arising from this

---

‡‡ I studied several books, pro and con, on this theory before committing to my position. Perhaps the best treatment is by Arthur C. Custance, *Without Form and Void*, whose details are provided in *For Further Reading*. It is, however, a highly technical study in Hebrew grammar pertaining to Genesis account. It's not light reading.

explanation of Genesis 1:2; however, this viewpoint also offers numerous satisfying solutions to many challenges often posed to Bible believers.

G.H. Pember in his classic work, *Earth's Earliest Ages*, digs deep into the Bible's language to draw out these amazing truths buried in the original wording of the Scripture. Pember argues, I think correctly, that the fossil record and many artifacts of intelligent life dating perhaps ten thousand or more years in the past are not necessarily from the current 'epoch' of humankind. They date from before the time of Adam's creation and the 'six days' of Genesis 1. We learn that there is also a Hebrew tradition from the Targum (an Aramaic version of the Bible and related 'commentaries' written during the second Temple period to the Middle Ages), that a 'pre-Adamite' race of humanoids existed. And their view was not alone amongst the ancients. Many other distant cultures possessed myths supporting this interpretation.

For instance, artifacts such as the ruins of Baalbek in Lebanon or Puma Punca in Bolivia, which may date from 10,000 to 15,000 BC, have been adduced by ancient astronaut theorists to prove 'extraterrestrials' have been here and were misunderstood by early humanoids to be deities. Pember would agree such relics and monuments attest to the presence of another form of intelligent life pre-dating the re-creation of the world and Adam's origination. It's possible another form of Homo sapiens existed with much of the same intelligent properties that *'Homo sapiens sapiens'* possess but without the *'imago dei' (God's image)* placed within Adam. Such predecessors to Adam would be reflected in the fossil record as we decipher it today. Likewise, cave art that dates from perhaps 35,000 BC forward, as well as other 'Stone Age' artifacts indicate a 'naked ape' with expansive capabilities but not the full equivalent of today's human being. Indeed, one of the great puzzles of anthropology is,

"Why have we witnessed civilization only in the past 6,000 years when scientists assume that the intrinsic capabilities of humankind (brain capacity primarily) haven't changed appreciably in the past 200,000 years?" The 'Gap Theory' as described here may possess a plausible explanation. When God created Adam, an additional capacity was added. This quality caused humankind to behave differently, eventually giving rise to civilization. It also made God directly knowable to human beings.

Therefore, it's possible that a different form of life lived on the earth contemporary to pre-Adamite humanoids. We don't know if these other life forms were extraterrestrial or angelic (or a combination); but what we do know is that God apparently begins with the current 'human family' in Genesis 1:2, moving forward from there.[§§] That is where 'our story' begins.

The Gap Theory of Creation doesn't necessarily conflict with *intelligent design,* today's popular and biblical response to Darwinism. Principles existing within the universe, testifying creation was designed with 'life on earth in mind,' would still be true. But Gap Theory does differ from *progressive evolution* (as espoused by some evangelicals and most liberal Jewish and Christian theologians).[***]

Likewise, *pure creationism* would conflict with 'Gap creationism.' Pure creationism asserts that the world and the

---

[§§] Richard Hoagland and Mike Bara, in fascinating book, *Dark Mission,* speculate that evidence for intelligent life in the form of 'cities' and architectures on Mars and the Moon suggest that humankind is a descendant of much earlier intelligent beings in our solar system. The 'face of Cydonia' on Mars looks quite human (if it is indeed artificial).

[***] This alternative view suggests that God worked through evolution; there is continuity from ancient times to the present. Most evangelicals would object for a variety of reasons, believing that science as well as biblical teaching is at odds with this notion.

universe are no older than Adam. Creationists assert that the earth was created with an appearance of age; and it's only 6,000 years old. Creationists contend scientific dating methods like 'Carbon-14' aren't reliable. Consequently, creationists can't accept the earth's actual age to be billions of years as science postulates. If Creationism is your view, I don't wish to fuss about whether you are right or wrong. However, I side with the 'Gap theorists' because I believe it better fits 'the facts' of what we find buried within the earth and yet, still allows upholding the infallibility and authority of the Bible. The issue is succinctly, *what does the Bible teach?* In my opinion Genesis 1:2 is better translated in accordance with Gap Theory.

Some would protest that Gap Theory is an accommodation to modernity and science (although we find it in many writings of Christian scholars throughout the last 2,000 year period – not just since the time of Darwin). Those who promote rigid Creationism maintain adhering to a 'young earth' is a test of orthodoxy. I disagree: The Bible can be interpreted either way; it most certainly is NOT a test of orthodoxy. There simply isn't enough clarity in what the Bible tells us about the timing of our origins to be dogmatic.†††

Another interpretative mistake: Misunderstanding Peter's meaning in his epistle regarding the "waters." We assume the overflowing of water discussed in II Peter relates to the flood of Noah. But this doesn't necessarily follow from the context

---

††† Even if we treat the account of Genesis as a 'mythical' story which affirms only that humankind is a special creation of God, I could still build my faith on that position. But the emphasis must be on (1) 'special creation of God' and that (2) humankind possesses the image of God in a unique way unlike any other creature that the LORD God made. The story tells us that humankind held a unique place in the world and communicates with God unlike any other creature in the Garden. There is a very special 'connection' between Adam and God.

of his argument. What Peter reveals is that God had created the old heavens and earth, but then (without explanation) the world was overflowed with water and life subsequently perished. The world became a chaotic wasteland. God had to recreate the world to make it capable of sustaining life once again. This actually suggests that there have been *two* global floods. That is, thousands of years before the Flood of Noah, another flood encompassed the earth. The flood of Noah is a much more recent catastrophe. Recall that evangelical scholars (who rely upon Bishop Ussher's calculations from the genealogy of Genesis), establish the date of Noah's flood at 2348 BC. The prior flood was at least 2,000 years before then, and logically could have been even further back in the 'annals of time.'

Peter's commentary reinforces the 'Gap' concept (in my interpretation) and, as stated above, employs this understanding as an analogy to undercut the arguments of scoffers who claim the promise of the Second Coming is preposterous. In essence Peter says to his readers, "Why pay attention to scoffers who base their point of view on a fallacious understanding of the creation. Because they don't understand how we got here, why should we care if they scoff about our where we're going? They base their understanding upon what they see. As such, they are without insight from God's revelation. They do not understand the past. Why should we rely upon them to predict the future?" Peter's argument implies God *intervenes* in space-time. Unlike the Gnostic notion that matter is too evil for God to handle directly, God 'touches' the material world. He directly alters the world we see. ‡‡‡

The issue we must consider, and in my examination what the Bible teaches, is that the *epoch of humankind* may be only a small, yet paramount parenthetical time period in an

---

‡‡‡ Of course, this is also why Gnostics could never accept a true incarnation (God becoming flesh), because flesh, being matter, is evil.

otherwise vast period of earth history. Might the earth be 4.5 billion years old? Yes it might, just as science says. But the context of the creation account in Genesis may only be referring to the past 10,000 to 15,000 years (or less, perhaps only 6,000 years) of that immense time span. If we accept the focus on the Bible is only *this final epoch* (from the moment of the 're-creation' of our world to the time Christ returns and restores the earth to a redeemed state), Peter asserts it makes the promise of His coming *even more certain*.

God has intervened supernaturally once before in a global and dramatic way to change the course of life on this planet. He can and will do so again. To understand the end, we need to correctly 'reckon' our beginning. Our destiny is made surer because of our origin.

FOR FURTHER THOUGHT: Does rethinking the possible 'creation' account enhance your conviction of Christ's return? If not, what does Peter's argument mean to you? How do you reconcile science's theory of our origin with what the Bible teaches? Has the 'truth of evolution' been a stumbling block for your faith in times past? Do you believe that those who teach the world is older than 6,000 years are unorthodox? Is "Gap Theory" (believing it or not) a test of orthodoxy? If Peter is saying God intervenes in our world, does this infer the Second Coming is consistent behavior for the 'Almighty?' Does this give you a strong reason to believe that God may intervene yet again in humankind's affairs?

12: Seeking the Identity of Antichrist

Let no man deceive you by any means: for that day [the Day of the LORD] shall not come, except there come a falling away first, and that man of sin be revealed, the son of perdition; Who opposeth and exalteth himself above all that is called God, or that is worshipped; so that he as God sitteth in the temple of God, shewing himself that he is God. Remember ye not, that, when I was yet with you, I told you these things? And now ye know what withholdeth that he might be revealed in his time.

For the mystery of iniquity doth already work: only he who now letteth will let, until he be taken out of the way. And then shall that Wicked be revealed, whom the Lord shall consume with the spirit of his mouth, and shall destroy with the brightness of his coming: Even him, whose coming is after the working of Satan with all power and signs and lying wonders...
(II Thessalonians 2:3-9)

THERE IS NO PROPHETIC TOPIC THE SUBJECT OF MORE BOOKS, BOTH SCHOLARLY AND SENSATIONAL, THAN THE ISSUE OF "WHO IS THE ANTICHRIST?" LIKEWISE, THERE is no matter more inclined to generate debate and speculation than the issue of, "How we can identify the 'Man of Sin.'" Movies have had a field day with the issue. We think of the 1960's cultural phenomenon *Rosemary's Baby* or the popular horror picture *The Omen* and its various sequels. Virtually every author who writes on the subject of the Antichrist offers extensive analysis on the matter – some even going so far as to name names.

It's interesting that the Bible nowhere instructs us to keep watch for the Antichrist. However, for many who study biblical prophecy, we dive into this search with both feet. Why do we do it? After all, is keeping an eye peeled for the 'Devil's Man of the Hour' really a good idea? Shouldn't we have genuine *misgivings*? For aren't we who call ourselves Christians *to watch for Christ instead*?

Although that is how the Bible explicitly directs us, nonetheless, many are swayed by curiosity and 'calculating the number of his name.' Indeed, logic drives the quest. We reason that once we detect signs of the Antichrist – drawing a bead on his identity – the return of Jesus Christ must be even more proximate. "Spotting the Antichrist" promises an early warning of Christ's return – *that is*, if you believe the *Rapture of the Church* happens *before* the Antichrist appears. Since a majority of evangelicals believe this to be the case, it's why many are so obsessed with identifying who 'the man of sin' likely will be. To lay out the argument:

1. In the passage of II Thessalonians, Paul leverages the connection between the appearance of Antichrist and timing of the Day of the LORD drawing a crucial conclusion regarding the order of these events. Paul describes the initial act of Antichrist to be "exalting himself above all that is called God, or that is worshipped." This action is 'officially' known as the 'Abomination of Desolation' as depicted by Jesus and before Him, as predicted by Daniel the Prophet (Matthew 25:15; Daniel 9:27). Antichrist declares his divinity inside God's Temple (most likely in the holiest place, known as the *'Holy of Holies,'* where the Ark of the Covenant – and on its top, the *Mercy Seat* – was placed in Solomon's ancient Temple). Antichrist's declaration is 'an abomination;' therefore, the declaration desecrates the Holy of Holies.

2. Going to the 'top of his argument' (verses 3 and 4), Paul indicates that 'the Day of the LORD' cannot precede the Abomination of Desolation. Because the Day of the LORD is specifically a time of judgment when God directs His wrath toward the unrepentant world, Paul wants to make it clear that the Antichrist shows himself before God releases His judgments. Subsequent to Antichrist's revealing (remember the *'apokalyptō* discussion' from Chapter 7), the judgments of the Trumpets and the Vials commence. We know this revealing of Antichrist happens exactly half-way through the 70th week of Daniel (see Daniel 9:24-27), kicking off the Great Tribulation. Therefore,

the world doesn't begin to experience God's wrath until sometime in the second half of the seven-year period.

3. Because Christians are to be saved from God's wrath and the inference is that the judgments of the Great Tribulation qualifie as *wrath from which we are saved* (we take this up in detail in Chapter 14), logically, the Rapture of the Church must happen *before* Antichrist is revealed.*

4. Like a logical syllogism, the thinking flows this way: (1) If we see signs the Antichrist is soon to be revealed and (2) we believe the Coming of Christ for His Church must happen sometime before Antichrist appears, then, (3) Christ's advent must be VERY SOON indeed.

Being a student of prophetic subjects for over 40 years, I've studied strong arguments for many Antichrist candidates. At one time, Henry Kissinger appeared to be the odds-on favorite. The movie, *Dr. Strangelove* strengthened His standing since the good doctor had a not-so-hidden resemblance to Henry Kissinger. Supposedly, the author of the screenplay had met Kissinger, an 'intelligence advisor' for the military, before HK was well-known. He foresaw how Kissinger would influence world politics in the years to come. At a minimum, this guess was astute. Kissinger's aggressive anti-communist stance and thick German accent dramatically enhanced his persona making him attractive not only as the role model for the eccentric Strangelove (the centerpiece of this outstanding cold-war political satire envisaging the nuclear apocalypse), but as a suspicious if not smart choice for Mr. AC as well.

---

* Pre-wrath advocates argue, 'No, the Rapture can happen after Antichrist is revealed, but it absolutely must happen before God's wrath commences.' Since the *Trumpets* and *Vials* may not take place until late in the final portion of the *Great Tribulation*, i.e., late in the final 3.5 years, the Rapture may finally occur with only a few months remaining in the 70th Week.

The three Antichrists of the French seer Nostradamus: Napoleon, Hitler, and a third persona (possibly tied to the mysterious *Mabus* of Nostradamus' quatrains), *fascinate many in our day*. As discussed in my previous book, *Mabus* as the jumbled name of the Antichrist appears to be a stretch, especially since many followers of Dr. No decode the name into familiar and current appellations like Bush, Hussein, and Obama. Therefore, if we select any one candidate over the others by trying to decode *Mabus*, our choice amounts to little more than a wild guess since no one truly stands out from the pack. Even if we could fathom Dr. No's meaning regarding Mabus, his other descriptions of the third Antichrist seem to imply Nostradamus didn't intend that *Mabus* represent the third Antichrist (See my chapter on Nostradamus in *Decoding Doomsday* for the details).

However, two books written during this past year provide substantial and compelling new information about Antichrist. One of those books written by Tom Horn is entitled *Apollyon Rising: 2012*. The other book, written by the late J.R. Church possesses the lengthy title, *Daniel Reveals the Bloodline of the Antichrist*. Both books yield rich historical analysis as well as fresh insights into the biblical material concerning Antichrist. For those interested, both books are 'must reads.' I provide only a summary and commentary here in this 'essay.'

Church's book studies the chapters of Daniel in sequence, interpreting Daniel's visions consistent with most other evangelical authors over the past 150 years. But J.R. adds remarkable insights from the church fathers of the third-century, including Irenaeous and Hippolytus. As one studies the quotations from these two third-century authors (direct 'descendants' of the teaching of John the Apostle and Polycarp, John's personal disciple), we become captivated by the consistency of their teaching (from almost 1800 years ago) with the writings of many Pre-millennial evangelical authors today.

In Irenaeous' book, *Against Heresies*, Book 5, Chapter 28, Irenaeous employs several common titles for Antichrist including the *Man of Sin*, a *man with fierce countenance* (attributed to the Angel Gabriel in his explanation of the *little-horn* of Daniel 8), and the *abomination of desolation* (so called by Christ in Matthew 24). Irenaeous also indicates it's likely the Antichrist springs from the *tribe of Dan*[†], quoting passages from the Old Testament books Jeremiah, Genesis, and the fact the tribe of Dan is not mentioned in the book of Revelation. Is Dan the Jewish forebear of the Antichrist? Many scholars think so.

From studying the Old Testament and several apocryphal books, we know that around 1400 BC when the Israelites conquered the land of Canaan, the Tribe of Dan settled near Mount Hermon (today's Golan Heights in Syria). This mountain marks the precise location where Canaan, a son of Ham, established his abode after the Flood of Noah. According to the non-canonical books of Enoch and Jasper, the peak of Mount Hermon identifies the location upon which angels "leaving their first estate" (see Genesis 6:4) descended to earth. A quick reminder: Supposedly, 200 angels, also known as 'the Watchers,' begat offspring with the daughters of men, which gave rise to the *Nephilim*. Moses, whom tradition holds as the author of Genesis, indicated the Nephilim were in fact the historical characters from which ancient mythology originated. As I've discussed elsewhere, since scholars generally designate these beings as demigods – part-

---

[†] One of the 12 sons of Jacob/Israel and original tribes of Israel.

human and part-god – we can describe them correctly as *chimeras*.‡

Thus, Dan located his people at ground zero. But for some undisclosed reason (perhaps because he realized his tribe lived at 'Spook Central' to quote a line from *Ghostbusters*), the **Dan**ite's didn't reside in this location for very long.§ Given the tribe of Dan was known for its sailing skills, Dan's descendants determined to leave their land in northern Israel and travel to the isles of Greece, where they became the **Da**naans (circa 1200 BC). According to Homer, it was in their ships the Greeks set sail to retrieve Helen from her lover Paris, the Trojan prince (circa 1000 BC).** While these details are amazing, the story relinquishes other fascinating facts.

Church cites strong historical records from sources such as Josephus and apocryphal books like *II Maccabees*. He indicates that following the Trojan War, a survivor named *Aeneas*

---

‡ We learn from Genesis and other apocryphal books that these Nephilim dominated the antediluvian world. Additionally, they may have been the primary reason that the Flood was brought upon the world, to destroy the 'mixed' blood of 'gods' and men. Only Noah was found "perfect in all his generations" such that he and his three sons (and apparently their 'sister' wives!) would restart the human race after the flood, to reassert the purity of human DNA.

§ Some scholars indicate that the Danites were unwilling to fight the Philistines to preserve their land. A lack of courage might have been the reason. If this is true, it becomes all the more remarkable that the Danites are destined to become the Spartans as we discuss later. As you may recall, the Spartans were known as the fiercest fighters of ancient times. It just goes to show that if you try to escape the lesson God wishes to teach, you best buckle down and learn it sooner rather than later. You can't escape the Almighty's lessons forever. He follows you, even to the Greek Isles!

** Helen was the 'face that launched a thousand ships.' Those ships were built by the **Dan**ites!

fled to the Italian peninsula after seven years of travel.[††] His progeny, the twins Romulus and Remus, founded Rome several generations later (approximately 758 BC). While generally regarded as purely mythical, the historian Plutarch assumed their historicity, remarking that Romulus was 53 at his death. Hence, we discern how through this progression of ancestry, the Romans may be in fact the offspring of the Trojan *Aeneas*; through his great grandparents the Greek Spartans; and from these forebears, the Jewish tribe of Dan. From Daniel's visions, Church identifies the 'little horn' and the 'people of the Prince to come' as both Greek and Roman. Therefore, the conclusion offered by Irenaeous and Hippolytus – that *Antichrist is a descendant of all three peoples* – finds classical, historical and biblical support.

In summary, Church's analysis of the bloodline of the Antichrist substantiates the traditional, historic viewpoint that 'the Beast' will come from European ancestry.

The other work that explores compelling new insights concerning his infernal highness is Tom Horn's *Apollyon Rising: 2012*. Horn also refers to various classical sources to demonstrate that the persona behind the Spirit of Antichrist is none other than the god, *Apollo*. The Bible certainly indicates the Beast is known as *Abaddon* in Hebrew and *Apollyon* in Greek. Revelation 9:11 says: *"And they had a king over them, [which is] the angel of the bottomless pit, whose name in the Hebrew tongue [is] **Abaddon**, but in the Greek tongue hath [his] name **Apollyon**."* Horn quotes several historians to demonstrate the connection between the names *Apollo* and *Apollyon*. But the evidence hardly stops there.

[††] Aeneas is the subject of Homer's *Aeneid*. Aeneas was a descendant of Dar**dan**us, the founder of Troy. The Dar**dan**elles also refer to this lineage as it is adjacent to the ancient city of Troy.

The case is made stronger still when one considers the various antichrist figures in history connected to Apollo. Indeed, the oldest *figure or fore type* for Antichrist is *Antiochus Epiphanes IV*, the Greco-Syrian king who reigned over Syria and most of what is today Iraq and Iran from around 200 BC to 166 BC. Antiochus and his descendants were the likely subjects of many of Daniel's very specific prophecies; plus, AEIV associated himself with Apollo. It was this king, Antiochus, who halted the ritual sacrifice of the Jews in Jerusalem in 170 BC, establishing an altar for Apollo in the Temple, and thereby desolating the Temple through this abomination.[‡‡] For three years, Antiochus' troops fought (and lost to) Matthias and Judas Maccabeus, ultimately leading to the liberation of the Jews – and the Jewish holiday *Hanukkah*. Moving forward in time, we learn how *Domitian*, the Caesar contemporary to John the Apostle (when John wrote his apocalypse), expressed a wish to be regarded as Apollo incarnate.[§§] But the Apollo connection doesn't stop there. Tom Horn indicates the name 'Napoleon' – one of Nostradamus' three Antichrists – actually means, 'the new Apollo.' (I would add another name to the list: Adolf Hitler who identified with the sun god Apollo through his ubiquitous use of the *swastika*, a Hindu symbol of the sun.)

Horn references several authorities in classic Greek studies who confirm that *apoleia*, the Greek word for 'perdition' (which Paul appropriates in II Thessalonians 2:3), is rooted in the name *Apollo* just as its spelling suggests. Therefore, the Apostle Paul equates the *Man of Sin* to the *Son of Perdition*,

---

[‡‡] In my previous book, I provided an illustration of a coin minted by this king bearing his profile on one side, while portraying Apollo – also known as the god of music, seen playing his harp – on the other.
[§§] Recall that Apollo is so named in both Roman and Greek mythology whereas *Zeus*, the highest Greek God and father of Apollo is renamed *Jupiter* in Roman accounts.

implicitly conveying the *Antichrist is the reincarnated Apollo.* I will mention other links later; but first, a minority report.

Considerable debate rages today surrounding several verses in the Old Testament which name the Antichrist 'the Assyrian,' proposing that the Antichrist will not originate from Europe (or America, Europe's former colonies in the New World). Instead, Antichrist will hail from the Muslim world. Isaiah refers to the Assyrian in several different passages. The first, Isaiah 10:24 says, *"Therefore thus saith the Lord GOD of hosts, O my people that dwellest in Zion, be not afraid of the Assyrian: he shall smite thee with a rod, and shall lift up his staff against thee, after the manner of Egypt."* Hosea also mentions the Assyrian (Hosea 5:13 and 11:5). Micah refers to the Messiah who will defeat the Assyrian when he says: *"And they shall waste the land of Assyria with the sword, and the land of Nimrod in the entrances thereof: thus shall he deliver [us] from the Assyrian, when he cometh into our land, and when he treadeth within our borders."* (Micah 5:6).

Some suggest the label 'the Assyrian' connects the Antichrist to *Nimrod.* Genesis 10:8, 9 comments concerning Nimrod's lineage: *"And Cush begat Nimrod: he **began to be a mighty one** in the earth. He was a mighty hunter before the LORD: wherefore it is said, 'Even as Nimrod the mighty hunter before the LORD.'"* ****

Nimrod founded the city of Babel (later, Babylon) leading the people to make bricks and create its famous tower 'reaching unto heaven.' His goal: Form a single government keeping everyone together in one place so that humankind might grow

---

**** Evidently, a popular saying in the time of Moses. Today, being a Nimrod means being stupid as Nimrod thought He could build a tower that would reach heaven. In ancient times, being a Nimrod likely meant being overpowering or visionary. As I am about to argue, being a Nimrod, biblically, means being a symbol of Antichrist!

strong. *"And they said, Go to, let us build us a city and a tower, whose top [may reach] unto heaven; and let us make us a name, lest we be scattered abroad upon the face of the whole earth (Genesis 11:4).* But the implication of his comment 'that we might make a name for ourselves' conveys something beyond strength alone. My sense: It suggests a striving to achieve equivalence in power to God or at least to the Nephilim who continue to reappear *after* the Flood of Noah. Aggregating everyone to maximize the power of humanity would support this goal. At minimum, it signifies how a united humanity forming a single 'state' can more forcibly work its will. We see this from the statement made by God that He must confound them lest they prove they can accomplish anything (Genesis 11:5-9). Consequently, we may regard Nimrod as a fore type of Antichrist. As he was an 'Assyrian,' it's certainly conceivable that the mention of *the Assyrian symbolically links to Nimrod* and implies Antichrist. Chuck Missler, one of today's most popular and highly regarded writer/teachers concerning Bible prophecy (from the evangelical perspective) proposes Antichrist could be called, 'Nimrod II.' Missler doesn't commit to this Islamic Antichrist, but proffers it as a possibility. My view: Rather than a literal Assyrian (coming from today's Iraq), the Antichrist as an Assyrian (the 'Nimrod' of the latter times and the Bible's depiction of him as an enemy of the Jews) *is only symbolic.* If this be so, it explains how the Antichrist could descend from Greek, Roman, and Jewish blood, yet *remains* pre-figured as *Nimrod.*

Going further still, other scholars connect the fact that Nimrod was the great hunter and in fact, it is he who is foreshadowed in the 'gospel of God in the stars.' It's certainly undeniable that the Egyptians connected the constellation *Orion the Hunter* with their god Osiris (believing Osiris and Orion were one and the same). Furthermore, the mythology of the stars suggests the Hunter *Orion* (Nimrod, aka Antichrist), is the enemy of Virgo (Mary) and her offspring (Jesus).⁺⁺⁺ Thus, from the 'original source,' Egypt, we see how Nimrod, Osiris, Orion, and Apollo all relate to the personage we know today as Antichrist. Is this conclusion supported by archeology?

Robert Bauval and Adrian Gilbert in their 1994 ground breaking book, *The Orion Mystery*, set forth a thesis that Osiris is the God celebrated in the famous Pyramids of Giza. The very layout of the Giza complex – notably the location of the three great pyramids – reflects the belt of Orion. Osiris is the sun God and is the same god that the Greeks and Romans named *Apollo*. As I documented in my previous book, it's this mythology centered on Apollo that occupies the cornerstone of pagan religions worldwide; it also lies at the center of that contemporary 'non-religion' religion known as Freemasonry. Many of the most sacred Mason symbols are clearly Egyptian (the *pyramid*, the *all-seeing eye* of Horus or Apollo, and the *eagle* – a contemporary replacement for the mystical phoenix).

Therefore, current scholars insist that Antichrist has been the subject of religious worship for over 5,000 years. He continues to be worshipped today in sophisticated, yet secretive halls of which we are not aware. ⁺⁺⁺ Because this is the case, does it not suggest the spiritual war between God and Lucifer

---

⁺⁺⁺ According to some scholars, even Freemasonry ascribes to the preeminence of Nimrod. Rather than identifying the origin of 'The Craft' with Solomon and his first temple, the most hidden of secrets known only amongst the 'inner circle' specifies that Nimrod is the real King of interest, and the Temple where the Craft began was actually the Tower of Babel.

⁺⁺⁺ Hoagland and Bara in *Dark Mission*, disclose how NASA is thoroughly captivated by Egyptian mythology, primarily because its principals are Freemasons. The mission to the moon was named *Apollo*. The new mission to the moon sponsored by George W. Bush in 2004 was named *Orion*. The 'Mission Patches' worn by astronauts featured the constellation Orion and highlighted the three stars in Orion's belt. But this only scratches the surface on NASA's fascination with Osiris.

is reflected throughout this universal religion and the count-less megalithic monuments we find across the world?   But the story goes deeper still.

Genesis says that Nimrod 'became a mighty one' – a *gibborim* – the Hebrew word for 'a mighty one.'   In Genesis 6:4, this word is used as well as Nephilim, suggesting that the two words are connected in some way. *"There were giants (nephilim) in the earth in those days (before the Flood of Noah); and also after that (after the Flood), when the sons of God came in unto the daughters of men, and they bare [children] to them, the same [became] mighty men (gibborim) which [were] of old, men of renown."*

This association leads Tom Horn to speculate that Nimrod was not only 'mighty' but may in fact have become a *demigod*, equivalent to the Nephilim.   Perhaps in a Faustian manner, Nimrod became 'more than mere man.'   His new found pow-er, supplied by the fallen angels described in the *Book of Enoch*, enabled him to emerge as the dominant leader of hu-mankind after the flood.   We are thus left wondering, "Was this 'becoming' a result of genetic engineering? Was he 'made into a mighty man' as a result of what the fallen angels ac-complished on his behalf?"   Was he a mighty hunter because of superhuman strength or stature?   This association between Nephilim, gibborim, and Nimrod has many authors today con-templating whether the Antichrist *may be more than a human entity.*   Is it possible that the Antichrist will have 'god-like' ca-pacities through an alteration of his DNA?   Perhaps, the prem-ise of *Rosemary's Baby* and *The Omen*, that the Antichrist is the 'seed' of Satan possessing Satanic DNA, isn't so far-fetched.

The Book of Revelation indicates it is this destroyer spirit, *Apollyon*, who reigns over the 'bottomless pit' and who is res-urrected possessing the 'Man of Sin.'   From the spiritual per-spective, there is no doubt that the Devil controls the Antichrist. But could the human possessed by this most evil of evil spirits also have demonic DNA as well? Horn takes the possibility even further, considering whether a genetic 'splice,' perhaps first applied to Antichrist, becomes the *Mark of the Beast.*

In my prior book, I examine whether Nietzsche's *übermensch* might be a modern description for Antichrist. In some ways, the Antichrist appears to be the literal fulfillment of Nietzsche's visionary 'superman.' [§§§] At the very least, in our day, Nietzsche's *übermensch* expresses this 'spirit of Antichrist'. He is a man who chooses his own values relying only on himself since he proclaims that God is dead.

But there are even more visual cues which may be considered. Horn mentions the connection between *Apollo and the wolf.*[****] He indicates that Herodotus, the 'Father of History,' writing in the 5th century BC, discussed a great people to the north of Greece known as the Hyperboreans,[††††] who worshipped Apollo and made an annual pilgrimage to the land of Delos where they participated in the famous Apollo festivals there. Lycia, a small country in southwest Turkey, also boasted a connection with Apollo, known there as *Lykeios, which ties to the Greek word Lycos* and means 'wolf.'[‡‡‡‡] 'Wolfmen'

[§§§] Certainly Hitler believed he was the fulfillment of the Messiah that many occult writers discussed late in the 19th century. Dietrich Eckhart, the spiritual father of Nazism according to Hitler, believed this literally. Hitler was quite committed to genetic engineering. He drew upon the poetic myths of the Nordic *Edda,* in which the purified Aryans would be supermen, no longer contaminated by Jewish blood.
[****] Horn, op. cit., pg.163.
[††††] Early on in his book, *The Antichrist*, Nietzsche has his Antichrist proclaim, "We are Hyperboreans." Nietzsche also called his followers Hyperboreans.
[‡‡‡‡] A strong case can be made that Britain is the island of Hyperborea. While Plutarch (writing in the 1st century AD) identified them as the Gauls, an ancient historian, writing 300 years earlier, Hecataeus of Abdera, identified this race as living on a northern island

are called *Lycans or lycanthropes* for this reason.§§§§ Apparently since *Apollo and the wolf* are connected, perhaps the wolf is an image we could associate with the coming Antichrist! In this context it's interesting to consider Jesus' teaching, *"The wolf comes to destroy. But the Son of Man comes to give men life abundantly."* (John 10:10, paraphrased).

With the science of *transhumanism* now appearing on the front page of our newspapers, coming as it were, to the foreground, we witness a frightening development. In laboratories today, scientists create chimeras just as depicted by H.G. Wells in his classic, *The Island of Doctor Moreau*. Likewise, the fear of Mary Shelly inherent in her novel *Frankenstein* reaches beyond a mere tale of horror. Should we create a new kind of human by altering our DNA, what manner of beast do we unleash upon the world?

---

bigger than Sicily with a temperate climate capable of growing all manner of crops. The North Sea was called the Hyperborean Sea. According to Hecataeus, the island also possessed a circular temple (which many scholars identify as *Stonehenge).* Interestingly, Stonehenge has been known as Apollo's Temple since classical antiquity (See Squire, Charles, *Myths & Legends of the Celts*, p. 42). It's a remarkable fact that supports the premise of the breath-taking book by Knight and Butler, *Before the Pyramids*, which provides compelling evidence that Stonehenge (built circa 3,000 BC) was based on Thornborough Henge (built circa 3,800 BC, in northern England), and that the Egyptian pyramids built 1,000 years after Thornborough Henge (in 2,800 BC) were in fact based on these henges. Thus, the Egyptian monuments were more sensational versions of what had already been created in England. (See Knight, Christopher, and Butler, Alan, *Before the Pyramids: Cracking Archeology's Greatest Mystery*, Watkins Publishing, London, 2009). Apparently, all three connect to Apollo. A thorough discussion of Hyperborea can be found in Wikipedia (see *en.wikipedia.org /wiki /Hyperborea).*
§§§§ The original search engines included not only Yahoo! but also **Lycos,** whose symbol was a dog.

The possibility exists humans may soon face decisions regarding our openness to scientific manipulation of our DNA (presumably) for beneficent reasons. It's entirely conceivable in a few short years government could demand the population receive some manner of genetic alteration as a vaccination against a horrendous plague, just as the movie *I Am Legend* portends. Alternatively, individuals in a marketplace where human attributes can be bought and sold – may opt to 'enhance' their genes in order to obtain super human capabilities. For the past decade ethicists and scientists have debated this possibility. Some are now calling for setting ground rules for this oh-so-serious game. So how should Christians respond?*****

At a minimum, we should recognize the matter of seeking Antichrist's identity takes on a completely new meaning. It's no longer solely a curiosity. It becomes a discreet means to detect the evil he represents and that inevitably looms ahead. Does this also suggest we should be trying to play a game of 'pin the tail on the donkey' by naming who the Antichrist is in today's world? I sincerely doubt it's a wise approach.

I subscribe to the view the actual human identity of Antichrist is unlikely to become apparent before Mr. AC reveals himself. Biblically, we may be able to discern his bloodline and build a case from what portion of the world he will arise. We can determine the Spirit of the Antichrist, but not Antichrist himself, not before he reveals himself. We must remember that Paul indicates Antichrist's revealing is an *apokalyptō*, something that stuns and surprises us. *Knowing the man's name before he 'confirms the covenant' with Israel and then desecrates its*

***** Look for a thoughtful Christian response to this question in the summer of 2011 from Defender Publishing Group, tentatively entitled, *Pandemonium's Engine*. I have the good fortune to contribute to the effort.

Temple, may be a fool's errand. And yet, deciphering the nature of the Antichrist spirit possessing him has surely been accomplished and made evident in these last days by such great works as offered by Church and Horn. Whether we call him Nimrod, Osiris, Orion, Apollo, Abaddon, Apollyon, or the übermensch, we know who that spirit resembles and what his agenda most likely entails. For now, that knowledge is enough.

Sir Isaac Newton, a great student of eschatology writing in the 17th century, admonished his readers to be alert and determine who this Antichrist might be. He wrote this directive in his 300 year-old English dialect (including all manner of strange spelling), "And therefore it is as much our duty to indeavour to be able to know him that we may avoyd him, as it was theirs to know Christ that they might follow him." ††††† Watching out for the 'Man of Sin' entails much more than engaging in obsessive study as prophecy enthusiasts. It's now an obligation for those who take the Bible seriously, believing our mission in this world demands we stand firmly against all manner of evil.

> *"For there shall arise false Christs, and false prophets, and shall shew great signs and wonders; insomuch that, if [it were] possible, they shall deceive the very elect"* (Matthew 24:24).

---

††††† And Newton continues, "Thou seest therefore that this is no idle speculation, no matters of indifference but a duty of the greatest moment. Wherefore it concerns thee to look about thee narrowly least thou shouldest in so degenerate an age be dangerously seduced & not know it. Antichrist was to seduce the whole Christian world and therefore he may easily seduce thee if thou beest *not well prepared to discern him.* But if he should not be yet come into the world yet amidst so many religions of which there can be but one true & perhaps none of those that thou art acquainted with it is great odds but thou mayst be deceived & therefore it concerns thee to be very circumspect." (Sir Isaac Newton, *Untitled Treatise on Revelation*, Section 1.1, *emphasis mine*).

FOR FURTHER THOUGHT: Can we face the prospect that the evil of Antichrist may appear incarnate in our generation? What preparation might be necessary if he were to appear in the years just ahead? Does learning about the Antichrist frighten you? Do you notice the German word über often today in popular discourse and the media? What does the meaning of übermensch convey to you? Do you agree with Newton's direction that we should know about him in order to recognize him when he appears? Have you recently heard of various political leaders being called 'the Antichrist?' Do you believe the Antichrist is alive today?

13: Date-Setting

And he spake to them a parable: "Behold the fig tree, and all the trees;
When they now shoot forth, ye see and know of your own selves that
summer is now nigh at hand. So likewise ye, when ye see these things
come to pass, know ye that the kingdom of God is nigh at hand. Verily I
say unto you, this generation shall not pass away, till all be fulfilled.
Heaven and earth shall pass away:
but my words shall not pass away."
(Luke 21:29-33)

WE HUMAN BEINGS ARE ALL ALIKE IN AT LEAST ONE WAY. WE LOVE DETECTIVE STORIES, MYSTERIES, PUZZLES, AND EXPOSING SECRETS. IT'S PART OF OUR DNA.

The books and movies of Dan Brown demonstrate how much we enjoy the intrigue of secret societies and uncovering the hidden facts of history. His novels, *Angels and Demons*, *The Da Vinci Code*, and *The Lost Symbol* effectively employ this powerful hook. Likewise, Brad Meltzer has written a number of mystery books on similar topics; it's led to his hosting an entertaining program on the History Channel: *Brad Meltzer Decoded*. Deciphering hidden symbols, cabals, even buried treasure are all subjects Meltzer has covered in these documentaries; plus, they're perfect examples of phenomenon which reach out and grab our attention.

It should surprise no one that those of us who are fascinated by prophecy are also chumps for stories based on such conspiracies. To prophecy buffs, foretelling the future has this same appeal, but *taken up another level*. Prophecy combines all of the aforementioned elements, plus it manifests the *supernatural*. Indeed, detecting the extraordinary enthralls us even more than plain ol' decoding. Additionally, when "we the faithful" personally witness prophecies fulfilled, it reinforces our faith and reminds us how our God is vitally at work in the space-time world: *Seeing means believing*. We conclude, rightly I might add: History happens *now* – right in front of our eyes, whenever we observe fulfilled prophecies. How can we avoid excitement when we witness it first-hand?

Those of us engaged in the study of Bible prophecy for several decades often recite numerous 'predictions' which have come to pass* (or are happening as we watch). Let's quickly enumerate the most prominent:

- The formation of the European Union and its growth will rival the United States in economic power.

- The American dollar will decline losing its hegemony in the world.

- Tens of thousands of Jews returned to the Jewish homeland, precipitated by the fall of the Berlin wall and the dissolution of the Soviet Union.

- Nations will move toward a one-world government and single currency; thereafter, a charismatic world leader will step to the foreground to take the reins of this government.

- The 'peace process' for Jerusalem and its neighbors will grow increasingly tense. An ever-escalating probability that Israel's surrounding neighbors will instigate a decisive battle in which they seek to destroy Israel and take its land.

- A Russian-Iranian alliance, without prior historical precedent, will be affirmed threatening Israel's survival.

- (Future) The one-world government will transact some form of treaty ensuring Israel's peace and security – a commitment for seven years. Mid-way through this period, a leader arises who first confirms the treaty then breaks it.

Of course, prophecy students single out that the most impressive historic sign of all lies with the formation of Israel in 1948. It was this event, formalized by the United Nations,

---

* These predictions are really interpretations of Bible prophecy as expounded by popular prophecy authors like Hal Lindsey, Tim LaHaye, Chuck Missler, Jack Van Impe, and Grant Jeffries. For the most part, however, these authors agreed with the interpretations offered here, forming a compelling consensus.

which proved the predictions of several Bible scholars from a century beforehand that the return of Israel to its native land was no metaphor.[†] The primary prediction in Ezekiel 35-37, highlighted by the classic passage known as "Ezekiel's dry bones" was literally fulfilled. For evangelical scholars who believed in a physical return of Jesus Christ, this event moved the prophecy countdown clock irreversibly to the *on* position. From this point forward, there is no turning back. All authors espousing the dominant Pre-millennial point of view consistently proclaim the return of Jesus Christ must come to pass *within a generation*. After all, didn't Jesus say that those who see these signs will witness His Kingdom come? *"So likewise ye, when ye see these things come to pass, know ye that the kingdom of God is nigh at hand" (Luke 21:28).* If the countdown began in 1948, then the length of a generation, biblically speaking, should disclose to us, vis-à-vis the 'outside (latest) date,' when Christ's return must occur. And yet, one essential question remains: "Does the Bible plainly identify such a specified length of time?" Many authors seem to think so.

A widely held view by prophecy pundits from the 1960's through 1980's rested upon the Bible's use of the term *generation. The definition most adopted* for a biblical generation included a *time span of 40 years.* This timing seemed certain. There are two reasons for such unassailable confidence:

1. First, Jesus predicted that within *one generation* of his death the Temple in Jerusalem would be destroyed (See Matthew

---

[†] I cite in my book *Decoding Doomsday* how Professor George Bush, a relative of the two Presidents, predicted this in 1843, approximately 100 years before it came to pass. But J.N. Darby, the founder of Dispensational Theology originating around 1825-35, is the most influential scholar and predictor of the literal return of Israel to its native land of Palestine. Bush may have followed Darby's lead. Not surprisingly, this view led many English Christians to support Zionism at the end of the 19th century.

24 and Luke 21). This came to pass right on schedule. Pontius Pilate crucified Jesus circa 30-33 AD. In 70 AD, the soon-to-be-Caesar Titus conquered Jerusalem and set fire to its temple. The Roman soldiers literally left no stone unturned as they eagerly sought the melted Temple gold which had seeped between the cracks of the massive stones.

2. Likewise, God judged the Hebrew generation escaping from Egypt (despite the faithful leadership of Moses) for failing to heed His commandment to go forth immediately to conquer the Promised Land. As punishment, this generation of Jews wandered in the Wilderness after the Exodus for 40 years, until *everyone in that generation had passed away.* Only those under 20 years of age could march into the Promised Land along with Joshua and Caleb. Even Moses was prohibited from entering due to one moment of indiscretion.‡

Consequently, with two such notable examples as precedent, most prophecy authors in the 1970's and 80's contended 40 years is the unimpeachable span of a biblical generation and a clear rule of thumb to establish how much time we have left before Jesus comes. Furthermore, assuming as most everyone did that the official formation of Israel in 1948 began the countdown to Armageddon; Jesus Christ's return in 1988 should have been a slam dunk.

Despite a quiet consensus of many evangelical authors, much criticism was leveled at outspoken Bible scholars who took this position. Most notably, many chided Hal Lindsey for arguing forcefully in the 1970's that *1988* was *the* date of Christ's return. By tying these two calculations together, he concluded biblical principles established 1988 as the *time limit* for all the prophesied events to transpire. However,

---

‡ Moses, out of frustration, struck the rock with his rod which God identified as the location of water He would supply to the Hebrews. God asked Moses only to 'touch' the rock.

Lindsey was hardly the lone voice in the wilderness making this particular prediction. A book released early in the 1980's entitled: *88 Reasons Why the Rapture Must Happen in 1988*, stirred the kettle as well. Some other Pre-millennial scholars jumped on the bandwagon. But 1988 came and went. The Second Coming didn't happen. What was wrong with the logic? After all, wasn't it derived from sensible biblical interpretation?

Probably not. If good scholarship had overcome the prophetic enthusiasm as it should have, authors would have discerned the Biblical generation can be *one of several lengths.* 40 years is not the only biblical guideline. For instance, Psalm 90:10 indicates a human life is set at 70 years, and perhaps by the strength of the life (or by God's grace), 80 years. *"The days of our years [are] threescore years and ten; and if by reason of strength [they be] fourscore years."* However, this is merely another example; citing the "biblical lifespan standard" doesn't establish the length of a "biblical generation" either. We must examine the Bible more closely to draw a reasonable and biblical conclusion.

Identifying the fault in the traditional logic begins by understanding the meaning behind the *two* biblical words translated *generation.* As you might guess, there's a Hebrew word in the Old Testament and a Greek word in the New. We know Jesus used the word "generation" many times in His teachings and proclamations. This word is written in the Greek New Testament as *genea* (pronounced, 'jay nay ah'[§]). It generally conveys "a whole multitude of men [humans], with the same characteristics, living at the same time." Jesus invoked this term over a dozen times in the Synoptic gospels (Matthew, Mark and Luke). Here are a few familiar examples:

---

§ Of course, our word **genealogy** comes from this root word. In English, it literally means the 'study of generations.'

- *"A wicked and adulterous generation (<u>genea</u>) seeketh a sign."* *(Matthew 12:39)*

- *"But whereunto shall I liken this generation (<u>genea</u>)? It is like unto children sitting in the markets and calling unto their fellows and saying 'We have piped unto you and ye have not danced and we have mourned unto you and ye have not lamented." (Matthew 11:16, 17).*

- *"The queen of the south shall rise up in judgment with this generation (<u>genea</u>) and condemn it." (Matthew 12:42)*

Furthermore, if we consider Old Testament uses of the Hebrew word for generation, *towlĕdah (pronounced, toe-lay-doth)*, the variability of the concept increases. Easton's Bible Dictionary recounts several examples of how "generation" is put to work in key passages of the Old Testament:

- Genesis 2:4, "These are the *generations*," means the "history."
- Genesis 5:1, "The book of the *generations*," means a family register, or history of Adam.
- Genesis 37:2, "The *generations* of Jacob" = the history of Jacob and his descendants.
- Genesis 7:1, "In this *generation*" = in this age.
- In Deuteronomy 1:35 and Deuteronomy 2:14 a *generation* is a period of thirty-eight years.**
- Psalm 49:19, "The *generation* of his fathers" = the dwelling of his fathers, i.e., the grave.
- Psalm 73:15, "The *generation* of thy children" = the contemporary race.
- Isaiah 53:8, "Who shall declare his *generation*?" = His manner of life who shall declare? Or rather = His race, posterity, shall be so numerous that no one shall be able to declare it...

** Easton, M. G. "Generation", *Easton's Bible Dictionary*, from *The Blue Letter Bible*. 1897. 24 June, 1996 31 Jan 2011. Note also: Sir Isaac Newton's study of ancient history suggested that classical Greek studies would show a generation being 33 years.

Thus, Easton concludes the Hebrews "reckoned time by the *generation*. In the time of Abraham a *generation* was an hundred years, thus: Genesis 15:16, 'In the fourth *generation*' = in four hundred years (see Exodus 12:40)."

Therefore, the first mistake eager prophecy advocates made during the past few decades rests in their becoming dogmatic about a particular length of time, i.e., identifying the Bible's generation as a timespan implying a specific length of years. We observed how examples exist for the timespan of a generation being 33 years, 40 years, 70 years, 80 years, and even 100 years. So to suppose that 40 years is the epitome of biblical generational timing is clearly flat wrong.

Consequently, on the first point of how long a biblical generation is, we could surmise that Jesus indicates a finite period of time bounded between 33 and 100 years. It's probably well less than a century but much more than three decades. Frankly, *striving for more precision than this is unbiblical.* Consequently, the gist of Jesus' message can only be summarized as a "timespan less than 100 years." When we come to His parable spoken within this Bible passage, Jesus powerfully makes this point. And yet, His parable is another example where frequent 'date setting' logic runs afoul, as we shall see next.

Jesus delivered a parable known as *The Parable of the Fig Tree,* to warn us (or better yet, *encourage* us) we should recognize *when* the time of His return is very near, even "at the doors." "*When they now shoot forth* (the leaves of the *Fig Tree* or **any tree** in Luke's version*), ye see and know of your own selves that summer is now nigh at hand.*" Most authors suggest this parable is actually an *allegory*, in which distinct elements of the story represent something "in real life." In this characterization, the *Fig Tree* represents Israel. Not long ago, on his web site Grant Jeffrey referred to an apocryphal story from the Gospel of Peter (written in the 2nd century) to argue the *Fig Tree* specifically refers to Israel. While he is correct the selection from this apocryphal account expressly confirms the common Pre-millennial viewpoint, from an interpretive standpoint (that is, from a *hermeneutical* perspective), we must ask, "Is this what the canonical gospels teach?"

Historic orthodox Christian tradition conveys that any and all allegorical interpretation is highly suspect. It may be proper to apply allegory to illustrate a truth, but not to determine it outright at the start. In other words, if you base doctrine on an allegorical interpretation you may wind up with egg on your face. Instead, the proper interpretative method avoids the notion of allegory altogether and sticks with the more modest concept of *analogy*.

This is especially so since other Bible scholars suggest that nowhere does the Bible use *the Fig Tree* as a symbol for Israel. If any tree is a 'figure' for Israel, the *Olive Tree is a* much better candidate. The prophets of the Old Testament compare Israel to an *olive tree* (See Isaiah 17:6, Jeremiah 11:16, Hosea 14:6). Even Paul's analogy comparing Israel to the Church, employs the *olive tree for the comparison, not the fig tree* (See Romans 11:17, 24). Hence, the point of the Jesus' parable is much less definite than Lindsey, Jeffrey and other of my 'pre-Trib' mentors propose. In other words, it's a mistake treating the parable as an allegory and connecting the "budding of the Fig Tree" with the birth of the political nation of Israel in 1948. This is simply "reading too much into" what Jesus is saying.

So does this mean that 1948 is unimportant? Not at all – it was a monumental date. But we would be smarter to think in terms of a progressive fulfillment of the Bible's prophecy of Israel returning to its land and reclaiming its heritage rather than identifying just one date. Indeed, if you recount the historical milestones, the resulting momentum is compelling:

- In 1896-99, the Zionist movement called for the nation of Israel to be reborn in the land of Palestine.

- In 1917, England conquered Jerusalem, winning it away from the Ottoman Turks.

- In 1917, Lord Balfour signed the so-called Balfour Declaration stating that the British Empire looked favorably on establishing a homeland for the Jewish people in the Middle East.

- In 1948, the UN partitioned Trans-Jordan to create Israel with specified borders.

- In 1967, the Six-Day War broadened those borders and included the retaking of Jerusalem by the nation state of Israel.

- In 1973, Israel ultimately won the Yom-Kippur War, which led eventually to peace with Egypt, and later Jordon.

- Since that time, Israel fought many other battles to solidify its land holdings and its security in southern Lebanon and Gaza.

In conclusion: By seeking to identify the precise date (so we can start a 'count-down clock'), we depart from what the Bible plainly states and enter the realm of speculation. Speculation is okay; but it needs to be labeled as such. Based solely on historical events of the 20th century, we can't be certain that any one date is the obvious 'kick-off event.' Likewise, another key expression Jesus applies in Luke 21:24, *"time of the Gentiles"* is subject to debate if we attempt to get too specific: *"And they shall fall by the edge of the sword, and shall be led away captive into all nations: and Jerusalem shall be trodden down of the Gentiles, until the times of the Gentiles be fulfilled."* A scholar of the caliber of the late John Wolvoord (1910 – 2002), former President of Dallas Theological Seminary and a strong voice in Pre-millennialism, believed the *time of the Gentiles* doesn't conclude until Jesus physically returns to earth and permanently restores Jerusalem to the Jews.

Nevertheless, Jesus' analogy is still very meaningful even *if* Israel isn't what Jesus intended by speaking of the Fig Tree. Indeed, the point of His parable is powerful: *Once the signs begin to happen, once there are blooms or buds, you can ex-pect the leaves to come forth soon thereafter. It's inevitable.*

Thus, what Jesus actually conveys comprises two distinct factors influencing how we understand the timing of His return:

1. In the first place, the signs will move forth with the same certainty as *buds lead to leaves*. That is nature's irrepressible pattern. It happens every year. There has never been a time when the summer leaves failed to come forth after the trees bloom – we can count on it. In this instance, we are being told, "Know this is a fact as certain as facts can possibly be."

2. In the second place, Jesus is saying, "Once this happens, there will be not be another autumn" (staying with His analogy). "Spring will be followed by summer. But summer *will not lead to autumn*. This summer is it. The leaves won't turn from green to fall colors again. The summer that follows after this particular *budding* is the last season we will witness. "

However, what is the *budding*? It isn't Israel becoming a nation per se. In context, it's only those signs Jesus recounts coming together *within one generation*. *"So likewise ye, when ye see these things come to pass, know ye that the kingdom of God is nigh at hand."*

At stake then, are two things: (1) "Have we properly interpreted the signs per the Bible's prophecies, signs for which we should be watching?" and (2) *if* we have rightly interpreted the signs, we must ask the hypothetical question, "Would God confuse us, allowing events not to run their course to the conclusion?"

Just to be crystal clear, Jesus underscores there is no way He will be deceptive about the timing of His return. Jesus' affirmative statement rules out any such possibility. *"Verily I say unto you, this generation shall not pass away, till all be fulfilled. Heaven and earth shall pass away: but my words shall not pass away."* How could Jesus be more emphatic?

He would never 'lead us down the primrose path' as my Mom used to say (quoting Shakespeare from *Ophelia*). We won't see the clouds gather and then, before the storm clouds burst, see them dissipate and clear skies return. Once the signs coalesce, once the clouds gather, the storm commences. Jesus exclaims with extraordinary emphasis, *He will not fool those who are watching!*

That leaves us with only the first issue: *Have we accurately interpreted the signs of His return?* Since many have been fooled in times past, we must conclude the fault lies not in God's faithfulness but in our ability to interpret His Word.

So the question we should ask is, "Have the predicted signs all come to pass within "this generation" as the Bible intends for us to understand that term? The answer is a resounding "Yes!" We should remember Jesus criticized the Pharisees for their failure to detect the signs of the times. If His point to them was 'interpreting the times in which they lived' should be obvious (and they failed to 'get it'), is it any less obvious for us? Would Christ's statement infer that knowing the signs of the times is confusing and complex? The opposite would seem to be the case. The signs must unmistakably spell it out.

I believe our generation is *the* generation which will witness the return of Christ Jesus. Can I predict it will happen in this decade? No. But isn't it absolutely mandatory it happen within the next few decades if Jesus words are to be vindicated? I believe the answer is even more emphatically "Yes!" This affirmation properly interprets the meaning of Jesus' words in Luke 21. Indeed, if we soft peddle the words and only casually affirm His soon return in the years ahead, we close our ears to the proclamation Jesus so forcibly uttered when concluding His message: *"So likewise ye, when ye see these things come to pass, know ye that the kingdom of God is nigh at hand. Verily I say unto you, this generation shall not pass* *away, till **all be fulfilled.** Heaven and earth shall pass away: but my words shall not pass away" (Luke 21:32, 33).*

The affirmative statement could not be more powerfully set forth by the Lord. He challenges us to understand His spoken words are so inexorable, so impossible to stop, we would more likely witness the entire universe collapse into nothingness than His words failing to come true. *"Heaven and earth shall pass away: but my words shall not pass away."* Jesus is adamant. His coming inevitably follows these signs – just as the leaves surely follow once trees break forth in buds.

Nevertheless, because we humans can't help but seek to know "the day and the hour" – insisting there must be a code that can be broken specifying the very day He is to return – we drift unavoidably *toward setting the date.*

The positive motivation behind our doing this derives from our faith in what we term *the providence of God.* For example, God has established the very stars in the sky in such a way to tell His story, as the old prolific scholar E.W. Bullinger (1837 – 1913) wrote.[††] Certainly, when that day comes, we will learn from the LORD why that particular date was chosen and then, how He foreshadowed it.

Yet, in the final analysis, setting a date refuses to abide in the key principle upon which our lives are based: *Faith. "The just shall live by faith."* (Romans 1:17) We seek to set dates because we lack faith. We know Jesus Christ will come soon. If we believe the signs have coalesced, we must insist Jesus comes soon, within our generation. To say less contradicts Jesus' very words.

However, striving to determine the exact date is a vain effort to set faith aside. For once we know the date – if that were possible – we would no longer need faith. While ironic, it's

---

[††] E.W. Bullinger, *The Witness in the Stars*

true: By trusting we can decode the date of Christ's return, we imply it's unacceptable to live by faith. We deny the faith we seek so earnestly to embody.

For this reason, along with the fact that setting a date (wrongly) will discredit the gospel as well as ourselves, we must resist the temptation. We can know He comes soon. But we can't know exactly when. We are obligated to live with that uncertainty as one aspect of the faith we are called to demonstrate to the unbelieving world.

FOR FURTHER THOUGHT: Do you believe confirming the 'signs of the times' strengthens your faith? Are you tempted to 'set a date?' Do you remember anyone predicting a specific date for the end of the world? What factors (signs) influence you the most when you contemplate how near we are to the 'end of days?' If an angel of God appeared and could tell you the day the world ends, would you choose to know or not to know? If you knew the Lord could come tomorrow, what would you do today? If you were to learn that He will come within the next ten years, what changes in behaviors would you likely put in motion? What action (s) should you take that is (are) consistent with Christ's admonition to "Look up for your redemption draweth nigh?"

14: Escaping the Wrath to Come

"And take heed to yourselves, lest at any time your hearts be over-charged with surfeiting, and drunkenness, and cares of this life, and so that day come upon you unawares. For as a snare shall it come on all them that dwell on the face of the whole earth. Watch ye therefore, and pray always, that ye may be accounted worthy to escape all these things that shall come to pass, and to stand before the Son of man."
(Luke 21:34-36)

WHEN TIMES ARE GOOD, IT'S EASY TO FORGET THE MASTER'S DIRECTIVE TO 'KEEP WATCH.' ON THE OTHER HAND, WHEN WE LIVE AMIDST THE 'WORST OF times,' there's a greater likelihood we turn our thoughts to heaven and consider the proximity of Jesus Christ's predicted return to this earth. In fact, when we find ourselves despondent about life's prospects, it's all too easy to wish that Jesus would "just come back right away and get us out of this mess" (a mess which we ourselves likely made without much help from anyone else!)

Most of us are not caught up in overindulgence at the moment. That's what the old word *surfeiting* means. In 2011, we struggle just to get by. Such is especially true for me and many of my friends who worked in the biggest and perhaps the most famous 'high tech' business in the U.S. (that one nearby in Redmond, Washington). Ten years ago we had plenty of money, we drove fancy cars, and we lived in big houses. Some in their 30's and 40's had already retired. However, today, houses in my neighborhood have fallen in value by 40%. Virtually everyone is 'under water' (that is, we owe more on our house than our house is worth). A lot of the youthful retired have had to go back to work. If you don't have any sympathy for 40-year-olds that have to go back to work, I can relate!

Looking at the bigger picture, financial prospects for America aren't so good. In Europe we see governments failing. In America, State and City governments, and even the Federal Government are struggling to balance the budget. Protests are becoming frequent. Some predict that riots aren't far behind. Perhaps the predicted financial collapse of the world (which contributes to the coming of Antichrist) is beginning at this very moment. Regardless, most everyone would agree that we aren't living in the good ol' days any more. Almost everyone yearns for better times.

Times are tough. I have to confess I've had desperate thoughts many times in the past couple of years. But one of the good things about these challenging stretches is that we're more inclined to contemplate the 'real meaning of life' in their midst than when times are good. We don't cling to material things. We may even be induced to pray, "Come Lord Jesus" to escape the circumstances in which we find ourselves.

It's not that uncommon for believers in the Second Advent to have such thoughts and comment accordingly. All too often, we hope to escape the bad times in which we find ourselves. However, in our better moments, we realize this escapism isn't the right reason to hope for Christ's coming. Although our personal circumstances may be dire, wishing for Jesus to come back trivializes what is in essence the culmination of history. Moreover, it's just a convenient means to a selfish end.*

Why is this so? I argue that by leaping to this 'way out' way out, we demonstrate *a lack of faith*. Jesus said He came that we might *"have life... more abundantly"* (John 10:10). That doesn't mean we will always have a *surfeit* of material goods. Neither does it mean we will only know peace and quiet. But it does promise that despite hard times, we can maintain our

---

* It's also interesting how this expression is usually uttered more often by men than women!

equanimity. Our outlook on life should remain positive because Jesus taught us to ask God to provide our *"daily bread."* Likewise, God shall provide *"all your need"* as Paul tells the church at Philippi (Philippians 4:19).

Yet, this assurance is a far cry from promising a Porsche for every garage. Indeed, perhaps the biggest heresy in Christendom during the past 50 years concerns the so-called 'Gospel of Wealth' which suggests all believers should prosper materially. Prosperity preachers teach we are doing something wrong if God isn't blessing us with wealth and health. Perhaps we have 'unconfessed sin' in our lives? Perhaps we 'lack faith?' I shudder when I hear such counsel. Indeed, I find this 'gospel' repugnant as well as unbiblical. Just consider the examples in the New Testament. When on earth, Jesus and His disciples had no more money than what Judas could carry in the common purse. The early Church shared possessions and conducted their 'church services' secretly in Roman catacombs and individual homes. Paul had to make tents lest he be a burden on his churches. Such outward signs do not convey great wealth amongst the faithful!

Nevertheless, weren't these believers living life 'abundantly?' You can bet they were. Being filled with the Spirit to the point of 'bursting' and witnessing miracles 'left and right,' they wouldn't have traded their new found faith and the joy they gained for all the riches in Rome. Consequently, it's neither a practical nor righteous motive, *hoping for the Lord's return to escape our personal bad times.*

So does this mean that when the *Last Days* are 'full on' (and the judgments of God are about to be unleashed upon the world), we just need to 'buck up' and deal with the horrible pressures and catastrophes the Bible predicts? Or is there something fundamentally different about these final days? As we approach the period known as 'The Great Tribulation,' no doubt our destiny in this scenario is one of the most momentous issues we face; therefore, we should study this matter in earnest.

Perhaps we'd rather not think about it. The less we know the better. On the other hand, shouldn't we examine whether we do have to go through the 'worst of bad times?' Will believers who trust in Jesus Christ live through the Great Tribulation?

If you're reading this book, you're probably a *Pre-Millennialist*. You also probably know what this awkward label means: You believe in a literal *Millennium Kingdom* in which Jesus Christ reigns physically on this earth for 1,000 years – just as *John the Revelator* predicts in the last book of the Christian Bible (if we take his words to be *literally true regarding their fulfillment in 'space-time'*).

It's interesting that John's discussion of this epoch is the only passage in the Scripture specifying the length of the Christ's earthly Kingdom will be a literal 1,000 years. It's also somewhat ironic that although the term *millennium* is never used in the Bible, it's the *key term we use to distinguish the various ways in which Protestant Christians interpret the meaning of the coming Kingdom.*

As a refresher (and for my readers that don't know), there are three protestant prophecy 'schools of thought:' The 'Pre,' 'Post,' and 'A' (pronounced 'Ah') Millennialists – reflecting a 'before,' 'after,' or 'not so relevant' perspective of when Christ comes vis-à-vis the Millennium. Today, most evangelical Christians are *Pre-millennial* while *Amillennial* best denotes 'reformation' Christian doctrine regarding when Jesus Christ (physically) returns to earth.[†] It's only been in the last 40

[†] Neither Martin Luther nor John Calvin, the preeminent reformers of the 16th century had much use for the Book of Revelation. They believed *Antichrist* was the Pope and the Catholic Church *was Mystery Babylon* as introduced in Revelation. That they didn't believe in a literal millennium shouldn't be surprising. Today's Covenantal

years or so that the 'Pre's' have outnumbered the 'Post's' and the 'A's.' [‡] We can thank Hal Lindsey's *Late Great Planet Earth* and Tim LaHaye/Jerry Jenkins' 'Left Behind' series of fiction books for fomenting this 'sea change.'

Hand-in-hand with the notion of the Millennium is the notion of the *Great Tribulation*. All *millennialists* (and some Christians that aren't into the Millennium), believe there will be a final period of time in which the earth will suffer the greatest distress it has ever known. Most believe this time period is equivalent to the Prophet Daniel's final (70th out of 70) 'weeks of years' (totaling 490 years of prophecy related to the God's plan for salvation of His people, the Jews). Daniel specifies that this last seven years of 'normal' history (in which humans apart of Jesus Christ 'run the show') consists of 2,520 days – that is, seven, 360-day years. Also, it appears the second half of this period, the final 1,260 days (aka 3.5, 360-day years) is particularly difficult. Known as the *Time of Jacob's Trouble* (so-called in Jeremiah's prophecies, see Jeremiah 30:7) and perhaps incorrectly as the Day of the Lord,[§] this period begins (as discussed in the last chapter), with the appearance of Daniel's prophesied *Abomination of Desolation*. This Abomination is the claim by the Antichrist that he is God – and he

---

Theology (J.I. Packer and R.C. Sproul, wonderful Christian authors and prime examples of this viewpoint), is strongly tied to strict Reformation views and consequently, Covenantal theologians often criticize those who hold to a literal Millennium in regards to eschatology.

[‡] I examine these various views, what underlies them, and ultimately, how our method of interpretation eventually leads us to the most biblical perspective. See my first book, *Are We Living in the Last Days?* for a thorough treatment of these topics.

[§] This phrase may refer to an even more specific period of time, perhaps days, weeks, or months, in which the final judgments of God are experienced by the inhabitants of the earth. This is either the same as the Great Tribulation or is a period of time at the very end of this 3.5 year period.

alone is to be worshipped by all the earth's people. According to the best scholarship today, it isn't until the Antichrist *proclaims himself to be God* and his self-declared worthiness of worship (specifically within the 'Holy of Holies' in a rebuilt Jewish House of Worship**) that (1) we know who the Antichrist is; and (2) we officially know the Great Tribulation has begun. Once this occurs, most scholars who believe in a literal return of Jesus Christ suggest this is the moment when the countdown to His return commences. After this amazing event transpires, we can calculate the exact day Jesus will return.††

Let's assume that the Abomination of Desolation (the forthcoming debut of the Antichrist) takes place sometime within the next decade or two. At that moment in time, a whole series of events commence including the issuance and enforcement of the *Mark of the Beast*, the appearance of *God's 'Two Witnesses'*‡‡ to preach against the Antichrist, and the miraculous ability of the False Prophet to make the image of the Antichrist appear anywhere in the world. In response to these events, God unleashes judgments against the Antichrist and those who accept his mark. These judgments are so destruc-

---

** This Jewish house of worship may be a rebuilt Temple or it might be a rediscovered ancient Tabernacle that is placed in the courtyard on the Temple Mount. Most scholars believe it is either the Tabernacle of Moses, or more likely, the Tabernacle of David that served as the shelter for the Ark of the Covenant until Solomon completed his temple (circa 1004 BC) and the Ark was transferred for what was intended to be its permanent resting place. It is thought the Third Temple won't be built after until the Messiah returns.

†† It will be 1,260 days according to the Prophet Daniel.

‡‡ Most likely these two witnesses appear in the spirit of Moses and Elijah. As John the Baptist was Elijah who came before Jesus to fulfill the Messianic prophecy (so said Jesus), these two personages will likely be distinct human beings but preaching and working miracles in the same power and authority as these two heroic figures of the Old Testament. The two witnesses will preach against Antichrist possibly for almost the entire 3.5 years of the Great Tribulation until they are murdered by Antichrist.

tive that most of the world's population is annihilated. Enormous geological processes will take place drastically re-shaping the topography of the world (mountains will be flattened, islands will disappear). Animals on land and fish in the sea will be virtually wiped out almost to the point of complete extinction. So the obvious question is, "Will Christians be here during this tumultuous time?"

The 'Pre-millennialists' have *three* different answers to that question. Here we encounter the next three 'sub-groups' with traditional but equally awkward labels applied by those engaged in the debate. There are the 'Pre-Tribers' 'Post-Tribers' and 'somewhere-in-the-middle Tribers.' This terminology relates to when the *Rapture of the Church* occurs and if so, precisely when it happens in relation to the Tribulation Period. Up front, we should remember that the term *rapture* in Latin means to 'seize' or 'snatch up.' This word *rapturae* is the Latin word Jerome selected to translate the Greek word *harpazo* when he created the Vulgate in the 4th century.§§ It is spoken in I Thessalonians 4:17, *"Then we which are alive and remain shall be **caught up** (harpazō) together with them in the clouds, to meet the Lord in the air: and so shall we ever be with the Lord."* *Harpazō* means *"to forcibly snatch out of the way."* Paul says in I Corinthians 15:52, *"In a moment, in the **twinkling of an eye**, at the last trump: for the trumpet shall sound, and the dead shall be raised incorruptible, and we shall be changed."* In other words, this event will happen faster than you can say "I'm going home."

Those that believe in the 'pre-tribulation Rapture theory' advocate for Christ to return secretly before the Tribulation begins and 'snatch' away His Church. The 'somewhere-in-the-middle Tribers' believe this happens after the Tribulation begins but before the actual judgments of God are *loosed*. That's

---

§§ The Vulgate is the Latin Bible of the Catholic Church.

why this theory is also known today as the 'Pre-Wrath' view. Advocates of the Pre-Wrath theory believe the 'Day of the Lord' – associated exclusively with the time of God's wrath – is a particular time period transpiring at the very end of the Great Tribulation (perhaps lasting 2 to 6 months). The final group, the 'Post-Tribers,' believe most Christians will face martyrdom although some will pass through the entire Tribulation period unscathed – until the exact moment of Jesus' return. Believers are 'translated' and immediately return with Christ to judge Antichrist and his armies at the Battle of Armageddon.

So which view is right?

We've already discussed the story of how Lot and his family were saved from Sodom and Gomorrah's destruction by God's angels entering into the city, collecting the family, and sneaking out before the break of dawn. Those that advocate for the *Pre-Trib* view believe this represents a universal biblical principle: *Before God sends judgment, He delivers His people.* In other words, His children do not experience His judgments.*** At the very least, we could say He puts His people in protective custody. Better yet, we should use an even more relevant analogy: Believers go into a witness protection program and are transported out of town altogether.

The Post-Tribers argue Christians have always been subject to martyrdom; we who are alive at the time of the Great Tribulation should not expect special treatment. Furthermore, Post-Tribers accuse the Pre-Tribers of *a lack of faith.* "You are looking for an easy way out" we might hear them complain. The implication is Pre-Tribers are cowards and won't face the persecution which appears inevitable in the days lying ahead. To Post-Tribers, the *Pre-Trib Rapture* is the 'great escape.' As a Pre-Triber myself, you might expect I'd be a bit upset by these

---

*** 'Discipline' yes – but 'judgment' no.

accusations. Well, perhaps a little. But my emotions aren't helpful to the debate. So how should we Pre-Tribers respond?

First off, it would seem appropriate to distinguish between 'human-inflicted' malicious acts such as torture and murder (aka *martyrdom*) versus 'God-inflicted' acts of punishment as depicted in the many judgments described in Revelation. As believers, we are told to expect persecutions. Certainly, it is considered a badge of righteousness to be seen 'worthy to be persecuted' for the sake of Jesus Christ. In the Book of Acts, we see this language spoken by those who are beaten and tortured for their commitment to the gospel of Christ (See Acts 5:41). But the accounts seem clear that such persecutions and even martyrdoms were not the acts of God, but of humankind. Christ's disciples don't blame God when they are stoned or thrown in prison by spiteful pagans.

Of course when it comes to determining who is right, the squabble between the Pre-Tribers and the Post-Tribers ought not to be settled solely based upon 'logic' but upon what the Bible teaches. Furthermore, accusations of one group targeting the other – questioning the quality of the other groups' commitment – should have no relevance to who's right and wrong. In logic class, we learn this is called an *ad hominem* argument. This occurs when the value of a premise is linked to a characteristic of a person. It's like saying, "You are wrong, because your mother wears combat boots!" Nevertheless, this type of sniping is commonplace and continues unfortunately today even among otherwise sincere Christians. In fact, the level of acrimony can be quite high, with one group speculating that the view of the other group is a heresy sure to cripple the proclamation of the gospel, today and perhaps in the Tribulation to come. Alas, we forget that Jesus said, *"By this shall all [men] know that ye are my disciples, if ye have love one to another."* (John 13:35) We forget we should never directly attack a person (or persons); *just the idea* with which we disagree. It's quite okay to *battle over ideas*; but not so commendable to wage war against others *personally* (especially our brothers and sisters in Christ) with opposing views.

What does the Bible say? There are numerous powerful verses which appear to state plainly that true believers *will be rescued from the coming judgments.* One such verse is from Paul's first letter to the Thessalonians: *"[We are] ... to wait for his Son from heaven, whom he raised from the dead, [even] Jesus, which **delivered** us from the wrath to come."* (I Thessalonians 1:10) Yet, this sounds like something that happened in the past and isn't relevant to the future. Doesn't this reinforce the view that we must pass through the Tribulation?

The key problem with the translation of the King James Version is that it incorrectly translates the Greek verb *'rhyomai'* in the *past tense.* 'Delivered' should be 'delivers' (implying present or future tense). Plus, according to the *Blue Letter Bible* the verb means "to draw to one's self, to rescue, to deliver." *Young's Literal Translation* of I Thessalonians 1:10, brings the meaning alive: *"and to wait for His Son from the heavens, whom He did raise out of the dead – Jesus, who is rescuing us from the anger that is coming."* The New American Standard Version provides a similar translation: *"and to wait for His Son from heaven, whom He raised from the dead, that is Jesus, who rescues us from the wrath to come."* The *Vines Dictionary of New Testament Words* provides this explanation:

> Here the AV [King James Authorized Version – AV] wrongly has "which delivered" (the tense is not past); RV, "which delivereth;" the translation might well be (as in Rom 11:26), "our Deliverer," that is, from the retributive calamities with which God will visit men at the end of the present age. **From that wrath believers are to be "delivered."** (Emphasis mine)

The passage employed as our epigraph for this chapter has something important to say here as well: *"Watch ye therefore, and pray always, that ye may be accounted worthy to*

escape *all these things that shall come to pass, and to stand before the Son of man."* (Luke 21:36) The key word used is the Greek Word *'ekpheugō.'* The word conveys "to flee out of a place" (such as prisoners escaping from prison). It does not mean "preserved through" the calamity, but being removed from it. *One is not removed from prison by being safeguarded in it.* The context of Luke's account strongly suggests the same thing: We are saved 'out of' the earth in order to *"stand before the Son of Man."* We must be taken out of one place to appear in another. God isn't into cloning.

Perhaps one of my favorite verses in this regard is I Thessalonians 5:9. I memorized it in college (as translated in the New American Standard Version) and it has stayed with me for 38 years: *"For God has not destined us for wrath but to the (full) attainment of salvation for our Lord Jesus Christ."* The King James Version says: "For God hath not appointed us to wrath, but to obtain salvation by our Lord Jesus Christ." *Vines Dictionary* explains what the word *'peripoiesis' (obtainment)* means in this context: "The act of obtaining" anything, as of salvation in its "completeness" – referencing this verse and II Thessalonians 2:14: *"Whereunto he called you by our gospel, to the obtaining of the glory of our Lord Jesus Christ."* The connotation is firm: *If you have it, you have all of it.* You will not be partially saved or 'saved' metaphorically. You will be *completely* saved. God intends that you receive all *the possible salvation you can get.* You will not be *left in the lurch*[†††] when God pours out His judgment upon the world.

[†††] A great phrase, whose origin is from the French board game of *lourche* or *lurch*, which was similar to backgammon and was last played in the 17th century. Players suffered a lurch if they were left in a hopeless position from which they couldn't win the game. Another possible origin: The lurch held casketed bodies awaiting a funeral. It was a small 'out building' sitting next to the Church. To be 'left in the lurch' would be a bad place to spend time, to be sure!

Once again, the context of I Thessalonians Chapter 5:1-11, clearly reinforces this same interpretation. Paul's admonition to his audience relates to *"knowing the times and the season;"* they are not in the *Day of the Lord* as they may have been assuming before he wrote. Study the context and it becomes clear this is the reason Paul penned his epistle. Paul teaches:

> ¹*But of the times and the seasons, brethren, ye have no need that I write unto you.*
>
> ²*For yourselves know perfectly that the day of the Lord so cometh as a thief in the night.*
>
> ³*For when they shall say, Peace and safety; then sudden destruction cometh upon them, as travail upon a woman with child; and they shall not escape.*
>
> ⁴*But ye, brethren, are not in darkness, that that day should overtake you as a thief.*
>
> ⁵*Ye are all the children of light, and the children of the day: we are not of the night, nor of darkness.*
>
> ⁶*Therefore let us not sleep, as do others; but let us watch and be sober.*
>
> ⁷*For they that sleep sleep in the night; and they that be drunken are drunken in the night.*
>
> ⁸*But let us, who are of the day, be sober, putting on the breastplate of faith and love; and for an helmet, the hope of salvation.*
>
> ⁹**For God hath not appointed us to wrath, but to obtain salvation by our Lord Jesus Christ,**
>
> ¹⁰*Who died for us, that, whether we wake or sleep, we should live together with him.*
>
> ¹¹*Wherefore comfort yourselves together, and edify one another, even as also ye do.*

Paul is explicit (paraphrasing): "Everyone calm down! We cannot be in *The Day of the Lord*. We would know if we were. Why? We would already be with the Lord!"‡‡‡ As Paul says

---

‡‡‡ Whether we are "wake" or "sleep" at this time, we shall *"live together with Him."* This is analogous to the language of the Apostle's

elsewhere, "*to be absent from the body is to be present with the Lord.*" (II Corinthians 5:8) We are to invoke these words to "*comfort yourselves together and edify one another.*"

In fact, Paul must remind them once again of this very same truth in his *next* letter, II Thessalonians. Clearly, the Thessalonians were obsessed with the prophecies of the Lord's Second Coming. Apparently, matters were made worse because the 'Post-Tribers' made the frightening claim *that all Christians were going to go through the Tribulation:*

> ¹*Now we beseech you, brethren, by the coming of our Lord Jesus Christ, and by our gathering together unto him,*
>
> ²*That ye be not soon shaken in mind, or be troubled, neither by spirit, nor by word, nor by letter as from us, as that **the day of Christ is at hand**.*
>
> ³*Let no man deceive you by any means: for that **day shall not come, except there come a falling away first, and that man of sin be revealed***, the son of perdition;*
>
> ⁴*Who opposeth and exalteth himself above all that is called God, or that is worshipped; so that he as God sitteth in the temple of God, shewing himself that he is God.*
>
> ⁵*Remember ye not, that, when I was yet with you, I told you these things? (II Thessalonians 2:1-5)*

Paul supplies his followers with a distinct clue as to how they can know whether they've missed the Rapture. It's really quite simple: *You will see the Antichrist reveal himself in the Temple of God, declaring himself to be God.* If you witness that, the Tribulation has begun! However, if you were found worthy to be rescued from the wrath to come and to stand before the Son of Man, you won't be here to watch this event (televised of

---

Creed: "We believe in the resurrection of the quick and the dead" – that when Christ returns He resurrects both those living at that time and those that have already died, i.e., are *asleep*. We are removed from the earth to "live with Him."

course) when it happens sometime in the future. Where will you be? Preoccupied – talking with loved ones in Heaven.§§§

Finally, Revelation 3:10 reinforces the very same concept yet again: *"Because thou hast kept the word of my patience, I also will keep thee from the hour of temptation, which shall come upon all the world, to try them that dwell upon the earth."* The King James Version uses the word *temptation* to translate the Greek word *peirasmos*. *Vines* indicates that a better English word for *peirasmos* would be 'trial.' The intention would be to 'prove something true or false,' as the remainder of the passage describes. The point is that God does not tempt humankind; but He sometimes tries us or tests us to prove (to us, not to Himself) *what He has said about humankind in His Word is true.***** Since this statement is made in the context of the book of Revelation, the testing that is coming upon the earth is extremely clear. It is tribulation highlighted by *great vials of wrath*. Jesus' promise excludes His own from such 'testing.'

To dig deeper: The promise of Revelation 3:10 was given to the church at *Philadelphia* (in ancient Turkey). Many scholars for the past two centuries have taught that each of the seven churches in Revelation 2-3 provide a prophecy related to seven historical periods for Christ's church; in other words, each church represents one of seven consecutive stages in church history. The Philadelphia church is thought to represent the church which lives immediately before the Lord returns. It's characterized by fervent evangelism and generally, orthodox teaching. The following verse, Revelation 3:11 begins:

---

§§§ Additionally, those of us that have had physical infirmities (I have an artificial left leg) will likely be checking out our new bodies. Remember that line in Isaiah, "The lame shall leap?" I plan to be doing some serious leaping! Amen and amen.
**** In this case, the lesson is likely that despite the severe 'testing' humans will curse God rather than repent. See Revelation 9:20, 21.

"Behold I come quickly." Thus, the context strongly implies that the Lord comes quickly to keep this church from the hour of trail that's just around the corner (and directed to the unrepentant world at large).

While I mentioned earlier the Bible *and not logic* should teach us the answer to the question of whether the Rapture of the church is before, during, or at the end of the Great Tribulation, it would seem appropriate nonetheless to point out two logical arguments *derived from Scripture* that suggest that the Pre-Trib position is correct.

First, there is the admonition of Jesus to *watch for His coming*. Many of His parables convey this sobering message. We are to be watchful and alert. However, if the coming of the Antichrist precedes the coming of the Lord – that is to say, if the Rapture doesn't happen until the moment of the actual Second Coming (the visible return of Christ to earth at the Battle of Armageddon) – logically we *should be watching for the Antichrist instead*. Once the man of sin appears, we know that we still have 3.5 years remaining before Jesus returns. The Antichrist's announcement would be the 'tripwire.'††††

But is this viewpoint biblical? I hardly think so. Not only is it out of character with the Lord's direct admonition, it's inconsistent with His statement that we *"know neither the day nor the hour"* of His coming. Once Antichrist appears, we *will know the exact day* of Christ's return.

Second, we are to comfort one another with the promise of His coming *to deliver us from the wrath to come*. If we know

---

†††† In my opinion, this is where the 'Pre-wrath' theory begins to collapse. Since God's wrath comes later in the Great Tribulation and Antichrist has already appeared at the mid-point, Pre-wrath theorists argue we will witness the Antichrist. Our blessed hope may still be three or more years away. If the Pre-wrath theorists are correct, we should be watching for Antichrist instead of Christ.

we must face the likelihood of martyrdom, the 'comfort factor' is dramatically diminished. Not only that, we would then face the fearful judgments and catastrophes that shall cause *"men's hearts to fail them for fear of what is coming upon the earth."* (Luke 21:26) This seems glaringly inconsistent with the Scripture and the nature of God's care for His children. We should be looking forward to the return of Jesus – not dreading the coming of the Apocalypse.[++++] Otherwise, our reward for studying 'what should soon come to pass upon the earth' would be a more thorough knowledge of how we may suffer. We might wish we were not so thoroughly informed!

To be honest, I wonder if the incredible challenge of God's performing the Rapture is simply something that we, dominated by our natural minds, can't comprehend. As a result, many believe it must be 'non-sense' because how could God suddenly 'translate' perhaps one billion bodies of the living and perhaps another two billion bodies of the dead – at the very same moment – from a corrupted (dead) or corruptible (mortal) state to an incorruptible (immortal) state. How could He do all that *"in the twinkling of an eye?"* Just directing the traffic alone would overload the circuits of the biggest computer we can imagine. But then, God is not a computer!

So if that challenge causes us to doubt, we should realize our problem is: "We *underestimate God's power to save."* God asks Abraham (and us) if we consider *"anything too hard for the Lord?"* (Genesis 18:14) I, for one, don't wish to suggest our God is incapable of anything. He remains *Elohim*, the Creator, as well as *Jehovah*, the covenant keeper. After all, what is the Rapture, but another stupendous act of creation,

---

[++++] See Appendix One and Two for additional arguments for the Pre-Tribulation Rapture; the first providing a series of additional 'logical' arguments and the second providing a discourse on the explicit meaning of the key word, *apostasia*, used by Paul to depict the Rapture.

converting a form of matter subject to decay to another which can never die or degenerate? Perhaps the Psalmist said it best when he exclaimed: *"[Such] knowledge [is] too wonderful for me; it is high, I cannot [attain] unto it."* (Psalm 139:6)

FOR FURTHER THOUGHT: Do we seek to escape circumstances by praying for Jesus' Second Coming? Do we believe the Rapture will really happen? Have you ever contemplated what it would be like if you are alive when it occurs? Do you remember the old bumper sticker, "Warning in Case of Rapture, Car will be Unmanned!"? Do you think such calamities as suggested by this bit of 'bumper-sticker theology' will happen? Will airplanes suddenly crash? Will machines go 'out of control' that were formerly operated by the newly translated? If God can't resurrect all of His children – both living and dead – in the 'twinkling of an eye' is anything too difficult for the Lord?

15: Knowing the End at the Beginning

The word of the blessing of Enoch, with which he blessed the elect and righteous, who will be living in the day of tribulation, when all the wicked and godless are to be removed... Concerning the elect I said, as I began my story concerning them: The Holy Great One will come out from His dwelling, and the eternal God will tread on the earth, [even] on Mount Sinai, and appear in the strength of His might from heaven... And the earth shall be wholly torn apart, and all that is on the earth shall be destroyed, and there shall be a judgment on all... And behold! He comes with ten thousand of His Holy ones [saints] to execute judgment on all, and to destroy all the ungodly [wicked]; and to convict all flesh of all the works of their ungodliness which they have ungodly committed, and of all the hard things which ungodly sinners have spoken against Him.
(Enoch 1:1, 3, 4, 7, 9)

ONE OF THE GREAT PLOYS FOR MYSTERY MOVIE PLOTS IS FORESHADOWING *THE END AT THE BEGINNING*, WHEN THE VIEWER CAN'T POSSIBLY KNOW HOW THE FORESHADOWING relates to the story as a whole. After this 'reveal' is complete (but without explanation to its meaning), the movie then 'goes back in time' to where the story really begins. At this point, the viewer becomes engrossed in the story (if it's a good one!). For the next two hours or so, the movie director does his or her best to make the viewer completely forget about what happened at the movie's outset. Once the finale arrives, the foreshadowing event appears unexpectedly. The viewer is shocked how the conclusion was clearly shown at the beginning; yet, the viewer didn't remember or relate what they saw 'early on' in the story as it unfolded. When this ploy is twisted just right, the viewer may be dumbfounded as to just how he or she was tricked by the director's story-telling genius. Being misled in this way makes for a great tale and a satisfying mystery movie experience. Believe me, I've been fooled more times than not!

One of the great mysteries in biblical studies is the place and value of the *Book of Enoch*. Like a good mystery plot, Enoch is a very old book (between 2,200 to 5,000 years old) which begins by providing information directed far into the future concerning *the end of the world*. The author addresses himself to 'the elect' – a rare phrase in the canonical Hebrew Bible as we will see. Moreover, what's so intriguing (if not ironic): Enoch speaks to those *living at the end of history* although Enoch lived *at history's beginning*. How could someone 'at the beginning' know about 'the end?'

The Book of Enoch has become a very popular book over the past 100 years. It's even referenced by Freemasonry. Sometimes we hear tell of a special type of magic: *Enochian* magic* – which as we will see makes reference to the god Hermes and the general magical system known as *Hermeticism*. Both systems of magic connect humankind to the religion of Egypt. Enoch, like Melchizedek (described as the Priest and King of Salem in Genesis and the Book of Hebrews) is indeed a mysterious character.[†]

The story and traditions surrounding Enoch are considerable. In some mythologies, Enoch is seen as the planner and originator of the *Great Pyramids of Egypt*. This theory suggests that since the pyramids were undeniably built before the Flood, the people who built the pyramids were not Egyptian. These traditions suggest the pyramids were known as the *Pil-*

---

* "Enochian magic is a system of ceremonial magic based on the evocation and commanding of various spirits. It is based on the 16th-century writings of Dr. John Dee and Edward Kelley, who claimed that their information was delivered to them directly by various angels. Dee's journals contained the Enochian script, and the table of correspondences that goes with it. It claims to embrace secrets contained within the apocryphal Book of Enoch." *See Wikipedia, Enochian Magic.*

† For inquiring minds, ancient Jewish wisdom, according to 'my' Rabbi, Daniel Lapin, asserts Shem, the son of Noah, was this priest.

lars of Enoch. Additionally, Enoch may have been the real person behind the god *Thoth*, the Egyptian version of the Greek god *Hermes*. Since Enoch was thought to be the originator of writing, this mythical god Thoth inherited this attribute supposedly creating written communication. With a small leap, the ancients came to regard him as heaven's *messenger*.

Many interpret Isaiah 19:19 in connection with Enoch. Their contention is the Giza pyramids were originally monuments to Enoch's God (and the God of Adam and Noah): *"In that day shall there be an altar to the LORD in the midst of the land of Egypt, and a pillar at the border thereof to the LORD."* The Pyramids lie upon the border which exists between Upper and Lower Egypt. Additionally, since they contain no hieroglyphics anywhere on their many vast inner or outer walls, some speculate their purpose was not to entomb mummies of the Kings. Instead they appear to 'encase' *ancient wisdom* – as their extraordinary dimensions incorporate mathematical knowledge about the world's geography – knowledge vastly beyond the grasp of early humankind.[‡] Even the notion of 'pi' (π – 3.14159...) appears intentionally constructed within the ratios of these megalithic buildings dating almost 3,000 years before Christ walked the earth.

However, connecting Isaiah's statement to the Egyptian pyramids may be a stretch given that the Giza pyramids existed at least 2,000 years before Isaiah, and since the context of Isaiah 19 infers a time far into the future when the Egyptians speak the language of Canaan (perhaps Arabic[§]?), are judged

---

[‡] See my discussion on the pyramids in my previous book, *Decoding Doomsday*, for specific information about this ancient knowledge.

[§] Arabic developed from ancient Aramaic (the language of Jesus and the language of 'Canaan'). Today, it is a melting pot of language spoken throughout most of the Middle East bequeathing many words to Spanish, Portuguese, and other European languages. As Alexander the Great enforced the Greek language upon most of the known world

by God, but then healed by Him. Along with Assyria, at this future time Egypt is under the authority of Israel (which has never transpired before). God speaks of all three peoples representing one-third of His entire earthbound family – reflecting upon the unity of all of Semitic peoples, specifically Abrahams' offspring, all of which were to be blessed by God.

Likewise, in today's discussions of prophecy, the *Book of Enoch* often pops up. As we will see, there are many absorbing themes in the book. We know it's quoted in the New Testament by both Jude and Peter. Yet, it's not a part of the Protestant or Catholic Holy Bible. The early church was clearly split on its authenticity and its position in the canon. Those who comment on it in our time suggest the book is much like Daniel and Revelation; that is, it's 'apocalyptic' in nature. It speaks about the horrible judgments which will come to humanity at world's end. Many of the so-called 'Church Fathers' treated the book as sacred; like Peter and Jude, they quoted the book in their writings. We find this true of Justin Martyr, Irenaeous, Origin and Clement of Alexandria. Tertullian (160 – 230 AD) especially considered the book to be Holy Scripture. Indeed, the Ethiopian Coptic Church preserves and upholds the book as part of its official canon to this day.

On the other hand, the early 'fathers' Hilary, Jerome, and Augustine challenged its authenticity. As a result, for almost 1,400 years the book was 'lost' to Western Christianity. It wasn't found again until a Scottish explorer, James Bruce, went to Ethiopia at the end of the 18th century upon hearing rumors of its existence there. Bruce brought back three copies of the book written in the Ethiopian language. Scholars suggest that the text was originally Aramaic and may have

---

in the 4th century BC, Mohammed and his followers imposed this language across the Islamic nations in the 8th century AD and forward.

been translated into Greek before being rendered into the Ethiopian language.

The first English translation was published by Richard Laurence in 1821. Another edition, more famous than Laurence's, was printed by R. H. Charles in 1912. Thereafter, a Greek text surfaced followed by an Aramaic version discovered in cave 4 at Qumran as part of the Dead Sea Scrolls in 1947.[**]

The book is traced to at least the second century BC and may have been written much earlier. In fact, there are suggestions by some, perhaps 'romantically,' that the book (or the first portion of it) was written by Enoch himself prior to the time of the flood. Some authorities considered Enoch to have been the first human to have developed the language known as 'proto-Hebrew.' As noted before, tradition indicates that he was the originator of written language altogether. We do know that the Proto-Hebrew alphabet was similar to early forms of Greek and Phoenician alphabets. Indeed, these three very ancient non-pictorial languages show many similarities (all three are based on symbols representing *sounds* rather than *pictures* as in hieroglyphics). These languages appear to date to at least 1650 BC. It's likely that *commerce* between the Greeks, Phoenicians, and Hebrews was the catalyst for the 'growth and development' of these alphabets, aka writing systems, during the centuries before King Solomon (who lived circa 1,000 BC).

If in fact Enoch wrote the original (or portions of it), this would push the dating back to 3,000 BC. As I've noted earlier, Biblical genealogy suggests the Flood of Noah occurred approximately 2,350 BC. If the Book of Enoch was on board Noah's boat, logically it would have been penned before that date.

[**] This recap is taken from Joseph B. Lumpkin's 'intro' to his version of *The Book of Enoch, a Transliteration*, and published May 2004.

So when was Enoch born and how long did he live? Jewish authorities suggest that Enoch was born in the Jewish year 622.[††] Moses indicates that Enoch lived for 365 years, and then 'God took him' (a mystery about which we will talk more in a moment). This would place Enoch's disappearance from the earth at about 988 in the Jewish calendar (around 3,000 BC).[‡‡] The Flood was about 650+ years later. Just for context, Abraham lived about 1,000 years after Enoch (around 2000 BC) and 1,000 years before Solomon. A simple ('rounded') timeline may help frame the chronology:

Adam's Creation	Enoch Translated	Flood of Noah	Abraham	Solomon's Temple	Jesus' Birth
4000 BC	3000 BC	2350 BC	2000 BC	1000 BC	1 BC

On the other hand, given the Christian New Testament quotes Enoch toward the end of the first century (probably around the time Jerusalem was destroyed in 70 AD), the book would have been known and revered well before that time, as inclusion in the Essenes' community confirms.[§§]

[††] Jewish dates begin with the birth of Adam in year one, which works out to our 4004 BC, according to a number of sources.
[‡‡] See *Dating Discrepancies in the Hebrew Calendar*, Sheldon Epstein, Bernard Dickman and Yonah Wilamowsky. This trio is composed of educators whose joint works on Biblical and Talmudic topics appear in *Tradition*, *Higayon*, and *Location Sciences*.
[§§] The Jewish sect that assembled the Dead Sea Scrolls circa 40 AD.

Therefore, although admitting it's a quixotic notion that the book was written by the actual Enoch, nevertheless it was certainly written well before the time of Jesus. Surprisingly, although written at least 200 years before the Christian New Testament, it foreshadowed the beliefs of the Christian community regarding events such as the Rapture, the return of Messiah with His saints, and the Great Tribulation at the end of time.

Was the book shared by Christians and Jews? Yes, but only for a time. Merely to speak of God *literally* 'walking on the earth', would disqualify the Book of Enoch from consideration by the Jewish Rabbis as they finalized their canon (in the second century AD, about 100 years following the destruction of the Essene community). To be more specific, the book smacks of a belief in 'incarnational theology' (that God could become man – something orthodox Jewish theology rejects) even though its setting is the antediluvian age. After Jesus and the rise of Christianity, Jewish scholars dismissed any notion that the Messiah could be divine. He was uniquely 'anointed' by God, but his essence was human and not divine.

Enoch's vision of 'the end times' is remarkable in that it confirms many of the main contentions Christians make about events of the Great Tribulation period and how the final act of humanity plays out. It's fascinating how it's specifically addressed to the *elect of God* who will be living in the 'end-time tribulation' when the world will experience great devastation. This notion of 'the elect' was a phrase used by Jesus and His apostles. As I mentioned earlier, it's so translated in the Old Testament in *only four places* and all of these are within Isaiah. Isaiah 42:1 states: *"Behold my servant, whom I uphold; **mine elect**, [in whom] my soul delighteth; I have put my spirit upon him: he shall bring forth judgment to the Gentiles."* This passage certainly refers to the Messiah and His mission to Gentiles. Here, the Messiah is seen as God's elect. But Israel can also be called God's elect: *"For Jacob my servant's* *sake and* **Israel mine elect**, *I have even called thee by thy name: I have surnamed thee, though thou hast not known me" (Isaiah 45:4). "And I will bring forth a seed out of Jacob, and out of Judah an inheritor of my mountains: and* **mine elect** *shall inherit it, and my servants shall dwell there. (Isaiah 65:9).* Likewise, another verse from Isaiah seems to refer to the Jewish people but at a very special point in time. *"They shall not build, and another inhabit; they shall not plant, and another eat: for as the days of a tree [are] the days of my people, and* **mine elect** *shall long enjoy the work of their hands" (Isaiah 65:22).* In all cases, we see the term *elect* referring to the Messiah or Israel during the Messianic Kingdom. For Enoch to begin his book 'to the elect' indirectly connects him to an audience living just before the Kingdom and therefore, at the time of earth's *Great Tribulation.* This is an indirect way to corroborate his direct statement regarding to whom he is speaking and at what time they live upon the earth. Consistency contributes to authenticity!

Enoch promises *the elect* that the ungodly will be eliminated altogether from the world. So stand strong! At this same time, God will walk upon the earth. Ten thousand saints (no doubt a number signifying a 'countless' contingent) will come with the Lord to execute judgment. In Jude, we read his reference: *"And Enoch also, the seventh from Adam, prophesied of these, saying, 'Behold, the Lord cometh with ten thousands of his saints, to execute judgment upon all, and to convince all that are ungodly among them of all their ungodly deeds which they have ungodly committed, and of all their hard [speeches] which ungodly sinners have spoken against him'"* *** (Verses 14, 15). Implied in this passage is the division of humanity into three distinct groups: (1) The Saints that come

---

*** Not surprisingly, taking the Lord's name in vain and doing evil in the name of God are extremely bad things to have on your record.

with the Lord; (2) the believing who will inherit the Kingdom; and (3) the unbelievers who will be taken out of the earth and cast into 'outer darkness' or into 'the lake of fire.' As such, the verse implies a particular cosmology of sorts at the end of time. Some of the elect have been transformed into 'Saints' and are capable of moving between heaven and earth. Some of the *elect* still live on the earth with 'standard equipment on board' – they haven't been transformed into immortal persons and are 'earth-bound.' Finally, at the beginning of the Kingdom, anyone who does not belong to this exclusive club – the *elect* – will be eliminated. The ungodly will not inherit the Messiah's Kingdom.

My wife frequently reminds friends that if they ever 'go to the mill, go with a *really bad person!*' What's her point? It refers to Jesus' teaching in Matthew 24:40-42: "*Then shall two be in the field; the one shall be taken, and the other left. Two women shall be grinding at the mill; the one shall be taken, and the other left. Watch therefore: for ye know not what hour your Lord doth come.*" The moral of the story: Better to be the one the Lord selects to enter into the Kingdom! This is not a good time to be 'outstanding in your field' – you may be left standing alone!

The passage in Enoch predicting how the '*Lord will come with 10,000 of His saints to execute judgment,*' repeats the same concept from other Hebrew prophets who also lived hundreds of years before the time of Christ.

Several examples:

- *I have commanded my sanctified ones, I have also called my mighty ones for mine anger, [even] them that rejoice in my highness. (Isaiah 13:3)*

- *Assemble yourselves, and come, all ye heathen, and gather yourselves together round about: thither cause thy mighty ones to come down, O LORD. (Joel 3:11)*

- *I saw in the night visions, and, behold, [one] like the Son of man came with the clouds of heaven, and came to the Ancient of days, and they brought him near before him. (Daniel 7:13)*

- *And then shall appear the sign of the Son of man in heaven: and then shall all the tribes of the earth mourn, and they shall see the Son of man coming in the clouds of heaven with power and great glory. (Matthew 24:30)*

It's also important that we learn the meaning of Enoch's 'mysterious vanishing.' While Enoch's book discusses many topics which we don't have time to cover here (such as the 'Watchers' and the 'Nephilim'), we will touch on *his disappearing act*. It reinforces several points we made in the last chapter.

One of Enoch's fascinating accounts is his 'whirl wind tour' of the earth from a flying vehicle. Enoch describes angels which escort him to heaven and guide him on this tour. Not only did Enoch travel around the world, we learn he also moved 'to and fro' between heaven and earth. Significantly, one of his rides was a one-way ticket to heaven. Only Elijah the prophet experienced the same type of trip – and his journey 'upstairs' was precisely in the form of a real *whirlwind ride* (II Kings 2:11). But don't be distressed: Neither experienced death!

We learn from both Moses and the writer to the Hebrews (tradition states the author was Paul the Apostle), that Enoch was a righteous man who walked with God. Because of this righteousness, God 'took him.' Paul says it this way: *"By faith Enoch was translated that he should not see death; and was not found, because God had translated him: for before his translation he had this testimony, that he pleased God."* (Hebrews 11:5) Just as the rapture is described as 'snatching up' or 'catching up' in the twinkling of an eye, so God's grab of Enoch seems to be an event happening in a split-second.

M.R. De Haan (1891 – 1965) was a great 'old-time' evangelical preacher, founder of the Radio Bible Class, and scholar who wrote many pamphlets as well as a 'mere' 25 books, many of which focused on the Second Coming of Christ. It was De Haan's view that Enoch embodied a foreshadowing of what happens to the Church (true believers) before the time of tribulation (aka, the *Great Tribulation*). Just as 'in the days of Noah' there will be three groups of people: (1) *God's people* which pass through the judgment (Noah and his family represent the Jewish people; (2) *unbelievers* who perish during the judgment (those who scoffed in Noah's time and again in the future Great Tribulation – who will be removed from the earth in an undesirable manner!); and (3) *believers* [the saints] who please God (like Enoch) and are translated before the judgment commences. Being righteous in God's eyes (since they embraced the salvation Jesus Christ offers by His substitionary atonement), they're been removed from the earth *before* the Great Tribulation – the time of judgment – which is equivalent to Enoch being 'taken' before the Great Flood in De Haan's analogy. As we've discussed many times before in this book, God removes His righteous ones before He sends judgment. Here is yet another plain example of God's preservation of His saints.

Few prophecies are the subject of as much derision as the concept of the *Rapture of Christians*. But the story of Enoch points out several interesting concepts that substantiate why the Rapture is no pipe dream:

- The Rapture is not without precedent. Enoch was 'taken' by God and did not experience death just as Elijah was taken up by the whirlwind. It has happened before. It can and will happen again.

- The translation of Enoch is connected to the Flood of Noah and should be included in the epoch Jesus implies when He speaks of *"As in the days of Noah, so shall it be in the days of the Son of Man..."* Both of these experiences are unique times of judgment. God is directly intervening in the affairs of men. There are many attributes that these epochs share, but a *rapture of the righteous* is certainly one of them.

• • •

- Enoch prophesies the coming of God, the Mighty One from Heaven, who comes to earth with ten thousand of His saints. It's intriguing and no small coincidence that *the first prophet to predict the Rapture was the first person to experience it.* Since coincidence is a word that doesn't exist in the Hebrew Bible, we can assume this connection is no coincidence either.

I could go on, but I've likely digressed too much already.

One of the Bible's most amazing psalms is *Psalm 139*. The psalm speaks of God's foreknowledge, His 'knowing beforehand,' about every aspect of our lives. God knows where we are all the time. We can't escape His presence no matter where we go in the world. Before we speak, God knows what we are going to say. Additionally, the Psalmist relates that God thinks about the Psalmist (King David in this case) far more than the Psalmist thinks about God! We read: *"How precious also are thy thoughts unto me, O God! How great is the sum of them! If I should count them, they are more in number than the sand: when I awake, I am still with thee"* (verses 17, 18). We learn our very form and features are all part of God's plan for us. Perhaps the most staggering thought is to learn God picked out a specific time in the history of the world for our life to be lived. The fact that we live during the 21st century is no accident. *"And in your book were all written the days that were ordained for me, when as yet there was not one of them"* (verse 16). God knows the 'book of our lives' from cover to cover. He knows how the story concludes before the moment we are born. Nothing is left to chance! And yet, we are free to make choices and are responsible for the decisions we make.

As we approach the final days of our lives on earth, especially as the times grow tougher and the ominous portents signaling the end become history, it's crucial we remember this amazing truth. Days gone by, whether easy or hard, are in God's pre-written biography of each of us. Today's experience is in the plan of God too. Likewise, the days which lie ahead are just as 'foreordained' as the moments already passed, moments we know in our heart testify to God's providence. Whenever despair or fear grips us, we should recall God has brought us each step of the way so far and will bring us the rest of the way home.

The Book of Jeremiah discloses one of the most comforting verses in the Bible. This book tells the story of a greatly revered prophet living just prior to the captivity of the whole Hebrew nation of Judah in the 6ᵗʰ century BC. Nebuchadnezzar, the King of Babylon, busied himself carting off the Jews to Babylon. This was not a highlight in Jewish history – it was the very worst of times. Yet, there was hope. The New American Standard Version translates Jeremiah 29:11 with these words: *"For I know the plans that I have for you, says the Lord, plans for welfare and not for calamity to give you a future and a hope!"* The King James Version brings a different sense to the meaning of Jeremiah: *"For I know the thoughts that I think toward you, saith the LORD, thoughts of peace, and not of evil, to give you an expected end."* However Bible translators choose to express it, the message is clear: God thinks about us constantly. God remembers His Plan. He continuously thinks good thoughts toward us assuring that our 'end' happens just as expected. God is our Father.

Perhaps the most powerful statement in the entire Bible illustrating that God's providence is a 'personal matter' concerns Noah's time spent in the ark. When Noah was being tossed to and fro by the greatest storm in the history of the world, as he was puzzling over whether the ark was sufficiently 'waterproof' and stout enough to withstand the raging tempest, he could have assumed the worst: Maybe God carefully oversaw the ark's loading but overlooked the treacherous voyage, forgetting about all the inhabitants within. After all, how could God's plan include the horrifically scary sounds, the creaking, and the threat Noah's ark would be torn apart? If Noah only considered his circumstances solely relying upon 'sense data,' it would have been logical to figure his family would face the same fate as the rest of humanity now drowned in the devastating flood waters beating up against his giant boat. But the Bible calmly asserts the basis for Noah's assurance: *"**And God remembered Noah**, and every living thing, and all the cattle that was with him in the ark..."* (Genesis 8:1).

"And God remembered Noah." The LORD was thinking about every creature, big or small, whether superbly human or a mere creepy crawler. He kept watch – making sure that each and every one was safe and dry. Just like Jesus said "every hair on your head is numbered" (Matthew10:30). God's providence is personal! Surely, Noah remembered God too and realized despite the fright the animals and his family experienced, they all remained safe, being held firmly in the arms of the Almighty God. Noah knew God's plan would not be thwarted.

God knows the end at the beginning. He sees the day we will join Him even if we can't see such a time in the midst of today's troubles. And God is fully capable of assuring, no matter what end He has in mind, it will come to pass exactly, in every detail, just the way He planned. That's why it's good to recall, despite the worst things we can imagine, nothing can confront us except first *God filters it through His fingers.*

As Paul reminds us in Romans 8:35-39,

> *Who shall separate us from the love of Christ? Shall tribulation, or distress, or persecution, or famine, or nakedness, or peril, or sword? As it is written, 'For thy sake we are killed all the day long; we are accounted as sheep for the slaughter.'*
>
> *Nay, in all these things we are more than conquerors through him that loved us.*
>
> *For I am persuaded, that neither death, nor life, nor angels, nor principalities, nor powers, nor things present, nor things to come, nor height, nor depth, nor any other creature, shall be able to separate us from the love of God, which is in Christ Jesus our Lord.*

To paraphrase Paul's admonition: Whatever we experience at this time or anything in the future is *powerless to separate us from the love of God.* We have that promise. As the days progress, we will be challenged to remember this promise even as God remembers each one of us. Likewise, we will not lack our daily bread, the provision He refreshes every day pledging to meet our most urgent needs. God is always attentive to His children. He knows the end from the beginning.

> *Remember the former things of old: for I am God, and there is none else; I am God, and there is none like me, **declaring the end from the beginning, and from ancient times the things that are not yet done**, saying, My counsel shall stand, and I will do all my pleasure (Isaiah 46:9, 10)*

God's plan 'will out' – whether we're talking the whole world – or just one small solitary life of His elect. God has a plan for each of us. And He continues to monitor that plan every day.

FOR FURTHER THOUGHT: Do we believe our lives are already anticipated by God fully such that despite what the future holds, He will lead us to the finish line? As the song, Amazing Grace expresses, "If God has brought us 'safe thus far'" will "He 'lead us home?'" Do we trust what God has in store for us? Has anything happened to you in these more turbulent times causing you to stretch your faith? Do you like living in times when your faith must be exercised? If you agree that God knows your future, does it encourage you to believe that He can help you endure no matter what may come? What are some of your favorite Bible verses or stories which assure you of God's love and plan for your life?

16: Obtaining the Glory of God

*For I reckon that the sufferings of this present time are not worthy to
be compared with the glory which shall be revealed in us. For the earnest expectation of the creature waiteth for the manifestation of the
sons of God. For the creature was made subject to vanity, not willingly,
but by reason of him who hath subjected the same in hope. Because
the creature itself also shall be delivered from the bondage of
corruption into the glorious liberty of the children of God.
For we know that the whole creation groaneth and travaileth in pain
together until now. And not only they, but ourselves also, which have
the firstfruits of the Spirit, even we ourselves groan within ourselves,
waiting for the adoption, to wit, the redemption of our body.
For we are saved by hope: but hope that is seen is not hope: for what a
man seeth, why doth he yet hope for? But if we hope for that we see
not, then do we with patience wait for it.
(Romans 8:18-25)*

BEFORE JESUS LEFT THE EARTH, NOT LONG BEFORE HE WAS
CRUCIFIED, HE GAVE HIS CLOSEST DISCIPLES, PETER,
JAMES AND JOHN – A GLIMPSE INTO THE KINGDOM.

Matthew introduces the story this way: *"For the Son of man
shall come in the glory of his Father with his angels; and then
He shall reward every man according to his works. Verily I
say unto you, there be some standing here, which shall not
taste of death, till they see the Son of Man coming in His kingdom."* *(Matthew 16:27, 28).* Chapter 17 in Matthew's gospel
begins immediately thereafter. The first event Matthew records in this new Chapter appears to fulfill what Jesus had
just predicted at the end the previous. We read:

> *¹And after six days Jesus taketh Peter, James, and John his
> brother, and bringeth them up into an high mountain apart,*
>
> *²And [He] was transfigured before them: and His face did
> shine as the sun, and His raiment was white as the light.*
>
> *³And, behold, there appeared unto them Moses and Elias [Eli-
> jah] talking with Him.*

4Then answered Peter, and said unto Jesus, "Lord, it is good for us to be here: if thou wilt, let us make here three tabernacles; one for Thee, and one for Moses, and one for Elias."

5While he yet spake, behold, a bright cloud overshadowed them: and behold a voice out of the cloud, which said, "This is my beloved Son, in whom I am well pleased; hear ye Him."

6And when the disciples heard it, they fell on their face, and were sore afraid.

7And Jesus came and touched them, and said, "Arise, and be not afraid."

8And when they had lifted up their eyes, they saw no man, save Jesus only.

9And as they came down from the mountain, Jesus charged them, saying, "Tell the vision to no man, until the Son of man be risen again from the dead."

I haven't preached many sermons in my day (I tend more to teach than preach), but one I was especially proud of was entitled, "The Prince in Paupers Clothes." It harkened back to Mark Twain's *The Prince and the Pauper*, a story about two boys who look alike, one the true Prince of Wales (Edward, son of Henry the VIII), and the other, a boy from a poor family. The boys meet and switch places to see if they can get away with the hoax. And they almost do, up to the end of the story when the switch is discovered and Edward is crowned King.

My point in the sermon was this: In His earthly life, Jesus was a prince wearing pauper's clothing until the day He was transfigured before His three disciples – when it was suddenly revealed to them *Jesus was the Son of God*, the voice of God Himself testifying to this truth. Jesus' glory was so stunning it seemed He shone like the sun! Furthermore, He was accompanied by two heroic Hebrew figures: Moses and Elijah, representing the two most important sections of the Old Testament and the Hebrew religion: (1) the Law and (2) the Prophets. To see Jesus in their company was an astounding confirmation to the disciples that not only was Jesus special, *He was superior to 'Moses and Elias.'* This snapshot of the three together reinforced the true identity of Jesus Christ. The fact He was glorified and shone bright as the sun, while Moses and Elijah apparently weren't similarly arrayed, inferred Jesus held a superior status. He enjoyed a glory neither Moses nor Elijah then possessed (later in this chapter, we will discuss when they may receive such a glorious appearance). The experience was so dramatic Peter didn't know what to say. Perhaps for their own protection (lest they be considered a bit off balance by every other follower of Jesus), the Master instructed them to keep what they'd seen to themselves until after they beheld Him, the Son of Man, risen from the dead.

The location of the event was most likely Mount Hermon. The mountain is part of today's Golan Heights, west of Damascus, rising over 9,230 feet. Scholars see this sacred landmark as the northern border of ancient Israel. The tribe of Dan resided at its feet until they set sail for the Greek Isles. As I explained in an earlier chapter, this mountain was the precise location where Canaan, a son of Ham, established his family after the Flood of Noah. According to the non-canonical books of Enoch and Jasper, angels "[left] their first estate" (see Genesis 6:4) and came to earth literally landing on the peak of Mount Hermon. Supposedly, soon thereafter 200 angels also known as 'the Watchers,' begat offspring with the daughters of men, giving rise to the *Nephilim* – a race of demigods.

It's not expressed in the Bible why Jesus chose this particular place for His transfiguration. But the 'coincidence' is telling. Indeed, most evangelical scholars believe it's because this location symbolized an *apex of evil*. By His transfiguration, Jesus reclaimed the ground formerly 'owned' (from a spiritual perspective) by the fallen angels. Israel's worship of *Baal* and *Ashtoreth* (a Hebrew version of *Ishtar*, the fertility goddess) 'in the high places' (inferring Mount Hermon) reaffirmed the mountain as the acquired property of 'the Evil

One.' It's fascinating conjecture to be sure; however, there is a bona fide historical basis for such speculation. Suffice it to say, the lesson of the story centers on this 'glimpse' into the Kingdom of God showcasing Jesus' glory, and positioning Him in the context of the Hebrew religion.*

More often than not, those rejecting the Christian gospel do so because they haven't heard the gospel presented in a biblical way. What they reject isn't necessarily 'the gospel truth' but their misconception regarding what the gospel means. In a similar way, too often the sound bites we throw out concerning how to *become* a Christian as well as what it means to *be* one, fall on deaf ears. To many our oft-repeated phrases regarding 'accepting Christ' have become meaningless clichés. In effect, our pearls have been trampled in the dust. Because our easy summations are meager and hollow sayings in the minds of many people, the meaning of 'receiving Christ' is not obvious to all those outside the circle of faith. We who attempt to share our faith in whatever manner we're called (and that should include all who call themselves Christian), now must work harder than ever to explain what's involved in coming to authentic and saving faith in the gospel of Jesus Christ.

Likewise, when it comes to 'fleshing out,' if you will, the concept of salvation, our notions are rather attenuated. There is much more than most of us realize. We understand we are

---

* It's also interesting that Moses and Elijah (Elias) appear with Christ in this vision. It's the considered opinion of most prophecy scholars that these two personages (Moses and Elijah) are either literally or 'in spirit' the two witnesses of Revelation 11. These witnesses oppose the Antichrist during the Great Tribulation period. At the end of their 3.5 year ministry they are murdered by Antichrist, but then are supernaturally resurrected in front of the entire world. This amazing event appears to take place 30 days before the Battle of Armageddon.

forgiven of our sins. When Jesus died at Golgotha outside Jerusalem, He took our sins to the cross with Him. *"He who knew no sin became sin on our behalf that we might become the righteousness of God in Him."* (II Corinthians 5:21, paraphrased). We also know that *"...while we were yet sinners, Christ died for us"* (Romans 5:8). This is indeed wonderful news. But it isn't the whole story we should fathom and share.

Evangelicals readily acknowledge *being saved* enables us to 'go to heaven.' We recall the famous passage that shrinks the essence of the gospel down to a single verse — John 3:16: *"For God so loved the world that He gave His only begotten Son, that whosoever believeth in Him should not perish, but have everlasting life."*

Moreover, the culmination of Christian salvation is actually one of our best kept secrets. There is so much more to the afterlife than we've been taught. And this lack of understanding is not a good thing. Our failure to fully appreciate what lies before us could be our undoing as we enter into these increasingly perilous times where we face persecution and all manner of difficulty. We do well to remember the epistles of the Apostles were written to their churches during times of turmoil. Being a follower of 'the Way' was not an easy task. The leaders of the early church armed the flock with a deep understanding of what was at stake. As we say today, their notion was truly a 'big idea.' For the most part, the early church stood up to the opposition even when it meant martyrdom. *We can be assured what they believed about the afterlife was a major factor energizing their amazing courage.*

That's why Paul prayed for his church at Ephesus with such intensity: He strove earnestly that they might fully realize what the salvation of God through Jesus Christ meant. He prayed that: *"The eyes of your understanding being enlightened; that ye may know what is the hope of His calling and what the riches of the glory of His inheritance in the saints"*

(Ephesians 1:18). He also prayed the same for the church at Colossae: *"To whom God would make known what [is] the riches of the glory of this mystery among the Gentiles; which is Christ in you, the hope of glory"* (Colossians 1:27). Today, more than ever, this astonishing truth is crucial to our Christian perspective: Not only are we made righteous in the eyes of God; but *the glory of God* awaits those who are adopted as His children. It's a wonderful and remarkable gift to have 'right standing with God' – but it's quite another matter altogether to possess *the glory of Christ*.

"The glory of God" – what does that mean? Are we really destined to be glorious like God? Will we really share in His glory? This seems incredible – to some perhaps even heretical. Does the Bible really say such a future awaits us?

Most everyone has at least a vague concept of eternal life. But the truth of the matter goes beyond clarifying that Christians (and orthodox Jews) believe in a bodily, physical resurrection. The historical Judeo-Christian view of heaven begins with an appreciation of our *corporeal* nature there. Jews and Christians believe 'having a body' is a good thing. This stands in contrast to (1) the classic view of the Greeks, and (2) the original Gnostics (familiar to us today through the publication of the Gnostic gospels of Thomas, Judas, and Mary Magdalene), as well as (3) today's variants to Gnosticism – occultists, theosophists, and advocates for the New Age. All of these religions, whether ancient or current, believe the afterlife implies existence as little more than a *ghost* – a spirit being that passes between 'this side and *the other side*.' They disparage the bodily resurrection because at the core of this universal pagan religion are these beliefs (1) matter is tainted with evil; and therefore (2) requires a less-than-pure being to handle matter; consequently, (3) the creation was formed by an imperfect 'middle-man' (be it the ancient notion of a *demiurge* or today's new idol implied in 'smart matter' or 'lively matter' as depicted in modern physics – a 'fantastic reality' allegedly explaining miracles and the supernatural). This 'worldview' is an explanation for *why evil exists* despite the assumption that 'God is good.' It's also a 'defense' for God's goodness – known as a *theodicy* – the classic (i.e., ages old) explanation for why evil exists in the world.

But Christians reject the notion *the creation itself is evil*. Instead, we believe an originally good creation was cursed because our sin (originating from humans and not God) altered what was initially made good.† Ultimately, both 'the sinner' and the creation are slated for full redemption by the Creator. In other words, the death of Jesus did more than pay the penalty for humankind's sin; it legally set the creation free to be made right again once Christ returns in glory. That is the meaning of Paul's argument in Romans 8:

> *For the creature [creation]* ‡ *was made subject to vanity, not willingly, but by reason of him who hath subjected the same in hope, because the creature [creation] itself also shall be delivered from the bondage of corruption into the glorious liberty of the children of God.*

In other words, God has a reclamation plan for our world and we are right at the very center of it! The creation in its entirety was subjected to futility for our sakes. This plan incorporates the essential gospel mystery. As Paul says, *"...we speak the wisdom of God in a mystery, [even] the hidden [wisdom], which God ordained before the world unto our glory"* (I Co

---

† Remember after every day (save one) those statements by God in Genesis – *"And God saw what He had made and said, 'It is Good.'"* This language was an emphatic rebuttal to virtually all other religions blaming evil on the creation. God's commentary is an unmistakable exclamation point for just how *good* it is!   God takes all manner of creation 'dissing' personally. He is the proud Creator.
‡ The word for *creation* and *creature* is one and the same: *ktisis*, (pronounced, *key-teh-sees*). Thus, it can be translated either way depending upon the context.

rinthians 2:7). While evil sought to wreck the creation due to our sin, God intervened in our world – in history – to redeem us and His creation. God planned from the beginning to bring good from what was corrupted. Paul goes on to say:

> *For we know that the whole creation groaneth and travaileth in pain together until now. And not only they, but ourselves also, which have the first fruits of the Spirit, even we ourselves groan within ourselves, waiting for the adoption, to wit, the redemption of our body.*

Once fully redeemed, we will overcome *"the bondage of corruption and obtain the glorious liberty of the children of God"* as quoted earlier. We are instructed this struggle was necessary to transform us into *glorified children of God*. For from the beginning, we were predestined to become like Jesus Christ:

> *For whom He did foreknow, He also did predestinate [to be] conformed to the image of His Son, that He might be the firstborn among many brethren. Moreover whom He did predestinate, them He also called: and whom He called, them He also justified: and whom He justified, them He also glorified (Romans 8:29)*

Salvation is a many-step process. Yet in God's eyes all the steps have already been accomplished. Though our experience today does not include the perfection we call *glorification*, nevertheless, we are told this next step is as good as finished (or as they say in my home Oklahoma, 'it's a done deal'). According to Paul's gospel, God 'called us' for this express purpose:

> *Whereunto He called you by our gospel, to the obtaining of the glory of our Lord Jesus Christ (II Thessalonians 2:14)*

In the Letter to the Hebrews, Paul lets us in on another secret. Somehow through the incarnation, Jesus Christ was *"made perfect"* through sufferings. This occurred despite the fact that all things were made by God for Him, and He Himself (the *Logos*) made all things. Through the process of the incarnation – *the experience of becoming human and living His life in a body like ours*§ – He was enabled to be the 'first-born' of many brethren, *"bringing many sons unto glory."* Paul refers to Jesus as *"the captain of our salvation:"*

> *For it became him, for whom [are] all things, and by whom [are] all things, in bringing many sons unto glory, to make the captain of their salvation* **perfect** *through sufferings. (Hebrews 2:10)*

What does Paul mean by being made *perfect*? He uses the term *teleioō (pronounced, tuh-lie-ah-oh)* – and repeats this word over ten times in the Book of Hebrews alone (and it's used repeatedly in the New Testament as well). Note: Paul is not inferring anything regarding the nature of Jesus – there is no hint He is less than pure or perfect in regards to sin. Rather, the term implies 'fully completed' in the sense that the goal was *achieved exactly as planned*. The word *teleioō* is translated 'fulfilled' in Luke 2:43 and 'finished' in John 4:34.** Think of its meaning as "mission accomplished." This word confirms God's plan is *predetermined* to be complete in all aspects. Our tribulations contribute to the process of being made into the glorious image of Jesus Christ.

> *By whom also we have access by faith into this grace wherein we stand, and rejoice in hope of the glory of God. (Romans 5:2)*

The Spirit of Christ, given to us as an 'earnest' (i.e., a down payment) commands this inner person (and ultimately outer person) 'makeover.' Visualize if you will, the following quotation from Paul:

---

§ Paul says, that Jesus was *"tempted in all ways just as we are yet without sin"* (Hebrews 4:15)
** It is similar to the word *teléo* (*tuh-lay-oh*), used in regard to Jesus accomplishing our salvation on the cross, with the words, "It is *finished* (*teléo*)" (John 19:30).

But we all, with open face beholding as in a glass the glory of the Lord, are changed into the same image from glory to glory, [even] as by the Spirit of the Lord. (II Corinthians 3:18)

Paul indicates the process has already begun. Perhaps the transformation we see today seems very minor; but it begins nonetheless while we live in our mortal bodies. *Our pains are purposeful.* And yet, Paul teaches the aches and pains we go through now are nothing compared to the enjoyment and wonder we will experience later. Why? Because God's glory will be revealed *in* us:

*For I reckon that the sufferings of this present time [are] not worthy [to be compared] with the glory which shall be revealed **in** us. (Romans 8:18)*

Paul provides a lengthy dissertation on these matters in II Corinthians 4: 16-18, 5:1-8. Let's review the entire passage together before I comment:

16For which cause we faint not; but though our outward man perish, yet the inward man is renewed day by day.

*17For our light affliction, which is but for a moment, worketh for us a far more exceeding and eternal **weight** of glory;*

18While we look not at the things which are seen, but at the things which are not seen: for the things which are seen are temporal; but the things which are not seen are eternal.

1For we know that if our earthly house of this tabernacle were dissolved, we have a building of God, an house not made with hands, eternal in the heavens.

2For in this we groan, earnestly desiring to be clothed upon with our house which is from heaven:

3If so be that being clothed we shall not be found naked.

4For we that are in this tabernacle do groan, being burdened: not for that we would be unclothed, but clothed upon, that mortality might be swallowed up of life.

5Now he that hath wrought us for the selfsame thing is God, who also hath given unto us the earnest of the Spirit.

> *⁶Therefore we are always confident, knowing that, whilst we are at home in the body, we are absent from the Lord:*
>
> *⁷(For we walk by faith, not by sight:)*
>
> *⁸We are confident, I say, and willing rather to be absent from the body, and to be present with the Lord.*

Paul begins by acknowledging even though our fleshly body is undergoing 'entropy' – it's running down and will eventually die and decay – our 'inner being' is continually renewed day after day (verse 16). Our inner being remains vital.

In verse 17, he remarks our afflictions amount to very little and are only temporary; nonetheless, they work on our behalf to create in us that which *far exceeds in value* the 'price we are paying' now. It's like a property which will last for all eternity – a "weight of glory" (the meaning of which we will discuss more in a moment). We are paying a small monthly rent now – but we will soon own a mansion, deed included, without any further payments due.

In verse 18, Paul reminds us: We must set our 'eyes' (to-day we would say, 'our focus') on eternal things *not seen*. For Paul, 'seeing is *disbelieving!*' We are to focus on what is eternal, what is seen 'with the eyes of faith.'

In Chapter 5, verse 1, Paul justifies directing our focus in this manner because our bodies on earth are growing older and running down minute-by-minute. But in heaven our eternal bodies are like houses that can't depreciate one penny.

In verses 2-4, Paul continues this analogy: We live in a dilapidated house now; we sigh and groan and hope for the day when we will obtain our 'new house.' It's not that we want to have no house at all – for we don't want to be found living without one. After all, *being naked* is an indication we don't have a new house 'to come home to' – perhaps because we didn't deserve one! Perish the thought!

In verse 5, Paul says not to worry. God's promise to us regarding owning a new house in heaven has been guaranteed by an earnest payment: He has given us *the Holy Spirit as a constant companion*. His Spirit in us confirms the house will be waiting for us to move in!

In verse 6, he switches subjects slightly, even lamenting a bit: While we live in the 'old house' we aren't residing in God's neighborhood! However, just as soon as we move out of the old house, we instantly move into the new one next door to where God is! (As a quick sidebar, Paul states, — *"Remember: We live by the truth of what we know, our faith, not by what we see"* – verse 7 paraphrased). He finally concludes this discussion by saying, "You know I'm so confident about this, I'd rather be absent from my body right now and be in my new house, in the new neighborhood, present with the LORD." Paul is brimming with confidence. Perhaps we should ask ourselves whether we concur with Paul's wish: *Do we believe our prospects to be so bright we'd rather change houses right away?* Or do we just want to cling to our old real estate?

At the beginning of this passage, we stumbled upon a mighty concept about what *glory* entails. Paul calls it "the *weight* of glory." What does he mean?

The word translated 'weight' in the Greek is *baros* (*bah-ross*) occurring six times in the New Testament. It's translated five times as 'burden' and only once as 'weight.' (See Matthew 20:12, Acts 15:28 for examples). The notion here is akin to saying how *we assign 'great weight' to an expert's remarks*. In effect, it's a matter of *authority*; yet possessing authority *with responsibility attached*. In another passage but within the same letter, Paul indicates how many of his opponents complained about his style. They criticized him as a weakling when face-to-face, but stern when admonishing others at a distance (through his letters). II Corinthians 10:10 says, "...

his letters are **weighty** *and powerful" (here Paul is mimicking his opponents).* The word employed in this verse is *barys*, an adjective form of *baros*. As an adjective, *barys* conveys not just sternness or severity *but strength and power.* His enemies were saying, "Oh, so you're a tough guy when you write, but when you're here in person you aren't so big and tough after all, are you?"

But if we have 'weight,' we aren't so easily intimidated. Our strength and 'presence' convey 'weight.' It's like boasting: "Don't mess with me! You're tugging on superman's cape!"

C.S. Lewis once wrote a book (as he was often inclined to do), entitled, *The Weight of Glory.* While he never actually refers to the text of II Corinthians in the book; this text is still his touch-stone. Christopher W. Mitchell says this, regarding what C.S. Lewis meant by "the weight of glory:"

> Lewis longed above all else for the unseen things of which this life offers only shadows, for that weight of glory which the Lord Christ won for the human race. And knowing the extraordinary nature of every human person, Lewis longed for and labored for their glory as well.[††]

Lewis was an evangelist. He wasn't always eager and enthusiastic to play that part. But he believed in the eternal value of the 'soul' who, on behalf of God, he sought. Goodness knows Lewis could look upon many he who attempted to convert, surmising that in their present state, they had no 'weight' at all. But the eyes of faith saw something very different. Lewis could see the potential in all humans in the same way Christ sees. Wright quotes Lewis from his book, *The Four Loves,*

> "But heaven forbid we should work in the spirit of prigs and Stoics," Lewis declared, writing of the ultimate purpose of love in

---

[††] "Bearing the Weight of Glory: The Cost of C.S. Lewis's Witness," Christopher W. Mitchell.

his book *The Four Loves*. "While we hack and prune we know very well that what we are hacking and pruning is big with a splendour and vitality which our rational will could never of itself have supplied. To liberate that splendour, to let it become fully what it is trying to be, to have tall trees instead of scrubby tangles, and sweet apples instead of crabs, is part of our purpose." In his fiction, theology, apologetics and correspondence Lewis can be seen hacking and pruning with the hope that his efforts might be used to produce "everlasting splendours."

Lewis understood very well what Christ won for us at Calvary was much more than forgiveness of sins – it was an amazing future life consisting of glory with 'great weight.' In other words, with the glory of God becoming part of our eternal natures, we will cease being 'light weights.' Our lives will carry a presence felt by other entities we will encounter in the Kingdom to come (be they mortal humans, angelic beings, or God Himself – to His praise and glory).

Perhaps we can't fathom what 'weight' our lives will convey then. We know we *are to rule with Christ* in the Kingdom that comes (*"and they lived and reigned with Christ a thousand years"* – Revelation 20:4). We are also informed specifically we will judge angels! (No doubt, to their chagrin since their might exceeds ours now – see I Corinthians 6:3.) We know after we're glorified, we're called "the Mighty Ones" in several passages (which we've cited earlier). We can surmise the "clouds of heaven" that accompany Christ are made white clouds not just because we are wearing white robes and command white horses. Somehow, our glory will shine forth too as we ride with Him. Our glory – God's ultimate gift through Jesus Christ via His death for us – will also contribute to the brightness of the shining clouds encompassing the heavens as the battle of Armageddon is joined.

No wonder the multitude that surrounds the throne in Revelation 4:10, casts their crowns before Jesus Christ. The Saints reflect who truly deserves 'their' crown. The glory which they possess was won by Jesus Christ, by His suffering on the cross. Indeed, for all but a few, our sufferings are meager compared to what He suffered on our behalf. And yet, He eagerly wants us to exchange our dilapidated 'house' for the *eternal house of glory* He has prepared for us.

Peter says in his second epistle that seeing the glory of Christ has made the promise of His Kingdom all the more certain. We read in II Peter 1:3-19:

> *Yea, I think it meet, as long as I am in this tabernacle [his body], to stir you up by putting you in remembrance;*
>
> *Knowing that shortly I must put off this my tabernacle, even as our Lord Jesus Christ hath shewed me.*
>
> *Moreover I will endeavour that ye may be able after my decease to have these things always in remembrance.*
>
> *For we have not followed cunningly devised fables, when we made known unto you the power and coming of our Lord Jesus Christ, but were eyewitnesses of His majesty.*
>
> *For he received from God the Father honour and glory, when there came such a voice to Him from the excellent glory, "This is my beloved Son, in whom I am well pleased."*
>
> *And this voice which came from heaven we heard, when we were with Him in the holy mount.*
>
> *We have also a more sure word of prophecy; whereunto ye do well that ye take heed, as unto a light that shineth in a dark place, until the day dawn, and the* **day star** *arise in your hearts.*

Peter bore witness that he saw Christ glorified "on the *holy* mount."[‡‡] This event comprised both amazing sights and confirmation that the prophecy of the coming Christ is now made

---

[‡‡] Signifying, by the way, that Christ *redeemed* this patch of ground in the process of His transfiguration. Peter can now call Mount Hermon *holy*. Could this be a foreshadowing of the redemption of creation that Paul discusses in Romans, Chapter 8?

even more sure. Peter's goal: Continue to strive, to "stir them up" (motivate them) until the day dawns when *the day star arises* in their hearts.

What is the day star? The Greek word is *phōsphoros,* the "bright and morning star." In classic mythology the day star means *the light bearer,* aka *Venus,* symbolizing in Peter's remarks the fulfillment of the glory of Christ arisen within us. Peter says (paraphrasing): *"I will continue to motivate you as long as I live and until the glory of Christ is shining in your hearts bright and clear like the morning star!"* How intriguing the 15th element, *phosphorus,* is an element that emits a glow on its own accord.§§ The presence of this element adds considerable *weight* to Peter's statement: It's an element contained within every human cell for all cell membranes contain its lipid form. It's the fuel used in explosives. It's also used in bleaches and laundry products to 'whiten' the load.*** Truly, it's a marvelous analogy of the glory that Christ possesses and what He eagerly awaits to impart to us.††† This

---

§§ The philosopher's stone – an agent catalyzing non-gold metals into gold, was thought to be composed of phosphorus in the 17th century. "In 1669, German alchemist Hennig Brand attempted to create the philosopher's stone from his urine, and in the process he produced a white material that glowed in the dark. The phosphorus had been produced from inorganic phosphate, which is a significant component of dissolved urine solids. White phosphorus is highly reactive and gives off a faint greenish glow upon uniting with oxygen. The glow observed by Brand was caused by the very slow burning of the phosphorus, but as he neither saw flame nor felt any heat he did not recognize it as burning." See *http://en.wiki-pedia. org/wiki/Phosphorus.*

*** Mark's account of the transfiguration uses this analogy: *"And his raiment became shining, exceeding white as snow; so as no fuller on earth can white them"* (Mark 9:3)

††† Some scholars believe that Adam and Eve were originally clothed in a manner of glory to some degree. Their bodies emitted light. When they sinned, in their fallen state the light ceased to shine forth and they realized they had 'lost their glow' and were naked. If true, God's

phōsphorus should *penetrate every aspect of our being* down to the cellular walls of our body, enlighten our natures as if we are *bleached from head to toe and set aglow*, and empower us from the 'explosiveness' of its substance. That is the manner of glory awaiting us. It is the glory of God.

However, until this transformation is complete, we have a job to do. Like C.S. Lewis, we must recognize the marvelous glory awaiting those *who call upon the name of the LORD* and are saved by His death. During the time that remains, we are challenged to 'grow the family' of God by seeking others – helping them realize the wonderful gift of His love and salvation. God is Love. And as we reach out to others, our own natures are made like His. The Apostle John shares this stunning insight:

> *Herein is our love made **perfect** [fully realized], that we may have boldness in the Day of Judgment: Because as He is, so are we in this world. (I John 4:17)*

As God is Love and His love transforms those who believe in Him, we too are meant to have our love *perfected* during this time. Our love is to transform others even as His love transforms us. God intends this for us now and until the day we are caught up to be with Christ. By having our love perfected (fully complete), we may be bold when we stand before Christ at the judgment for believers.*** Finally, we are to acquire the

---

clothing for them was to hide the fact that they no longer had this 'sheen.' It's also quite similar to the story Paul tells of Moses after he visits God on Mount Sinai. The account says Moses' face glowed after encountering God's glory. We learn in the story that Moses was forced to cover his face because this glow frightened the Hebrews. Deeper scholarship suggests, however, the glow eventually wore off and Moses kept the covering to hide the fact that he no longer emitted the glowing sheen he once had! (See I Corinthians 3:7-18)

*** This judgment is not the 'White Throne' judgment of Revelation 20:11 (expressly for unbelievers) but the so-called *bēma* seat of

keen eyes God has for all those who surround us. We are to see them as prospective fellow heirs to the glory of God.

Our love is to be motivated by *this weight of glory!*

FOR FURTHER THOUGHT: When asked to describe what salvation means, what words do we use? Do you believe that the glory of God is meant to be shared with His children? How are believers worthy to be glorified? How does glorification motivate you to live a 'holy life?' Does the metaphor 'weight' add to your understanding of what 'glory' entails? Does this strengthen your motivation to withstand temptation and hardship? Are you encouraged to share God's love with others? Is our inspiration enhanced when we understand what manner of afterlife those who do not believe stand to lose?

Christ (*bēma* referenced a low platform from which civil judgments were made in the Roman Empire). *"For we must all appear before the judgment seat (bēma) of Christ; that every one may receive the things [done] in [his] body, according to that he hath done, whether [it be] good or bad."* (II Corinthians 5:10) Vines comments: "At this *bēma* believers are to be made manifest, that each may "receive the things done in (or through) the body," according to what he has done, "whether it be good or bad." There they will receive rewards for their faithfulness to the Lord. [But] For all that has been contrary in their lives to His will they will suffer loss."

APPENDIX ONE:

Logical Reasons to Believe the Rapture Comes before the Return of Christ at the Battle of Armageddon (Implying a Time Interval)

Implied in the 'Coming of the Saints' as described by Joel, Jude, Enoch, and Paul is that the *Saints* (all who believe and have accepted Jesus Christ as their savior) come from heaven, not immediately from the earth at the climatic time of Jesus' return to fight the Antichrist at Armageddon. Logically, if they come from heaven, the Saints first have to leave the earth behind. This implies a gap of some length between these events. But there are many other factors which also infer a necessary gap of time to fulfill Bible truths.

As a reminder, there are essentially three groups who believe in the Rapture but differ as to when it occurs. Group one believes it happens before the final seven years, Daniel's 70th Week, aka *The Great Tribulation*. Group two believes it happens no earlier than half-way through this period of time and precisely before God unleashes His wrath upon the earth. The 'gap' between the Rapture and the Second Coming may be a few months to a few years.* Group three believes that the Rapture and the Second Coming happen at virtually the same

---

* This is also a view that suggests that Jesus first returns to Jerusalem and takes ten days to fight battles throughout the area surrounding Jerusalem before concluding these 10 days in the Valley of Megiddo – at the 'Mount of Megiddo,' aka Har-megiddon. These ten days may be the fulfillment of Jewish holiday period known as *The Ten Days of Awe* between Rosh Hashanah and Yom Kippur. If true, *Rosh Hashanah*, the Feast of Trumpets, is when Jesus returns visibly to the entire world while the Battle of Armageddon transpires ten days later on Yom Kippur, known by Jews as the Day of Judgment. This is discussed in David Busch's book, *The Assyrian* (See *For Further Reading*).

moment. Jesus returns for His saints a 'split-second' before His Saints then return with Him to fight the Battle of Armageddon. This last battle occurs at the very end of the seven years. My argument here should find support from groups one and two, while being challenged by group three. The third group, those that believe the Rapture happens immediately before Christ physically returns to judge the ungodly (the 'post-tribulation' view) must address some logical challenges as follows:

(1) Why don't the biblical accounts of the Rapture include the detail of 'translation and judgment' happening simultaneously? This sequence seems rather significant. These actions are never spoken of by Jesus or Paul as concurrent events. If they actually transpire a split second apart, that's quite an oversight. Additionally, since there are so many references to this event it's remarkable that never once do any biblical statements tie the two events together.

(2) If there are other events such as the 'judgment seat of Christ'[†] where each believer's 'works' are judged after they are resurrected (or raptured). Does the 'judgment seat of Christ' also happen in the same instance as the 'translation and the judgment of the unrighteous?' That would mean *all three events occur in the same moment*. Again, each action is clearly spoken of separately by New Testament authors and by Jesus in His parables. There's no insinuation they happen concurrently, 'in the twinkling of an eye.' Paul depicts the Rapture occurring in a split second; but do all these other events happen consecutively in the very same instant?

[†] See Romans 14:10 and II Corinthians 5:10. This is the *bēma* seat judgment as mentioned in the final chapter.

(3) Perhaps the following objection shouldn't be considered since I may be 'thinking from a human perspective.' I offer it nonetheless: When do the Saints get their 'marching orders?' If we haven't first gone to be with Christ, wouldn't we be a bit overwhelmed with the transformation to immortal beings in one second, being judged by Christ in the next moment, and then returning with Christ to judge the unrighteous one second later? To be 'Mighty Ones' we should be equipped with knowledge of our powers, duties, and 'the battle plan' well-rehearsed.

(4) If Christ has gone to prepare a place for us (remember that *mansion in the sky?* – See John 14: 2, 3); when do we get to check out the real estate? Is it only the 'dead in Christ' that died before the Rapture who inherit a mansion? Are raptured believers left out? Don't the 'raptured' (aka, the 'quick') obtain a mansion too?

(5) With all these staggering events and wonderful experiences crowded together, there's no time for a celebration! There's no 'homecoming' – no party with that 'great cloud of witnesses' that has been cheering us on. (Hebrews 12:1) We've been waiting for this momentous day all our lives only to discover, there's no opportunity to appreciate what's just happened? This would certainly be poor planning and frankly, not in character for our Father in heaven. I doubt the LORD overlooked a celebration for us. After all, He's always been big on feasts. Just look at the Mosaic Law and all the Jewish 'holy convocations' (*holidays* – there are seven of them if you care to count). All are times of remembrance and rejoicing. Christ often compared His coming to a feast. Our God enjoys sharing wonderful occasions with His people.

(6) Next, we are promised *a time of rest*. We are to live worthy lives so we might enter into that time of rest. Paul says, *"Let us labour therefore to enter into that rest, lest*

any man fall after the same example of unbelief" (Hebrews 4:11). But with all these events happening so
quickly, 'one, two, three' it sounds like we must 'get to
work' immediately. Is there 'no rest for the weary?'

(7) If the Rapture occurs at the same instant that Christ returns *physically* to the earth, then no 'humans' exist to
inherit the earth. All believers have just been raptured
– and all unbelievers are eliminated. How do humans
enter into the Millennial Kingdom when none are left on
earth? The description of the Kingdom plainly indicates
human beings dwell on earth and are ruled by Jesus from
Jerusalem (See Ezekiel 40-47). Note: the same phenomenon would have happened if Noah and his family had
been translated as Enoch was. Noah's offspring had to
remain on earth to repopulate the earth. Otherwise, the
righteous would have been all been *snatched up* and all
unbelievers would have been destroyed in the Flood.
That's why believers converted during the period known
as the Tribulation (equivalent to that class of humanity
who refused to accept the Mark of the Beast), are analogous to Noah's family, and become the 'starting point' for
repopulating the earth. These believers 'missed the Rapture' and were *left behind*, so to speak, but became believers during the Tribulation; and therefore, inherit the
Kingdom of Christ as mortals. Once again, these mortals
will be asked to 'replenish the earth.'

(8) Lastly, we've established the premise that God removes
His righteous servants before unleashing judgment. This
was discussed in several chapters in this book notably in
the discussion of Lot and the example of Enoch. The example of Noah is disqualified for reason number seven
above. If this principle is rejected, then those who believe
otherwise must offer a rebuttal demonstrating why this
principle is 'the exception and not the rule.'

APPENDIX TWO:

The Greek Word *Apostasia* and its Implications for the Rapture of the Church

*"Let no man deceive you by any means; for that day shall not come, except there come a **falling away** (apostasia) first, and that man of sin be revealed, the son of perdition (apoleia)"*
(II Thessalonians 2:3)

While we've discussed a number of arguments for the 'pre-Tribulation Rapture' – that Christ returns for His Church sometime before the Tribulation period (or at least before the wrath of God is unleashed upon the world) – there is another argument to consider that hangs entirely upon the meaning of the Greek word *apostasia*, which is often translated, 'falling away' in the manner of an apostasy. Certainly, the Greek root for the word 'apostasy' – *apostasia*, is rather obvious. The English word *apostasy* is translated as "the renunciation of a religious or political belief or allegiance, typically in the sense of moving from an orthodox or traditional position to a heterodox or non-traditional view." But is there a sound argument the word *apostasia* can mean something other than 'a falling away' or 'apostasy?'

Because of the English definition, accompanied by a common interpretation and translation of the Greek word *apostasia* in most versions of the Bible, it would appear a stretch to consider any other alternative. In context, Paul's message has normally been understood as 'the Antichrist cannot appear, until an apostasy comes first.' Given the Antichrist is referred to in this passage as 'the MAN OF SIN' and 'SON OF PERDITION' (remembering the linkage discussed earlier between the word translated 'perdition' [*apoleia* in Greek], and the Greek / Roman god *Apollo*, the destroyer god), it seems logical to interpret *apostasia* in this way.

However, there are a number of evangelical scholars who argue forcefully that the better English word to express *apostasia* lies with the word *departure*. If this word is the more accurate translation, it would enhance the pre-tribulationist view. The passage would read, *"Let no man deceive you, for that day cannot come unless a departure comes first, in order that the son of perdition can be revealed."*

Terry James, editor of a recent book on various prophetic topics, entitled, *The Departure*, cites Dr. Thomas Ice, a top scholar on biblical eschatology who "presents well-researched thought on the term 'departure'" as well as Gordon Lewis from his paper, *"Biblical Evidence for Pretribulationism,"* * and how this affects the passage in II Thessalonians 2:3 and by implication, the timing of the Rapture. Quoting Lewis:

> The verb may mean to remove spatially. There is little reason, then, to deny that the noun can mean such a spatial removal or departure... The verb is used fifteen times in the New Testament. Of these fifteen, only three have anything to do with a departure from the faith (Luke 8:13; I Timothy 4:1; Hebrews 3:12). [Otherwise] The word is used for *departing from iniquity* (II Timothy 2:19), from *ungodly men* (I Timothy 6:5), from *the Temple* (Luke 2:27), from *the body* (II Corinthians 12:8), and *from persons* (Acts 12:10; Luke 4:13). (Emphasis added)†

Terry James points out a series of other authorities and cites their research into the meaning of the term. One selection in particular quoted by James of a Dr. (Wayne) House is helpful:

---

* See *Bibliotheca Sacra,* (vol. 125, no. 499; July 1968) pg. 218.
† Quoted from Terry James, editor: *The Departure*, Defender Books, Crane, MO. From the essay, "In the Twinkling," pg. 369. Originally published in *When the Trumpet Sounds: Today's Foremost Authorities Speak Out on End-Time Controversies* (Eugene, OR: Harvest House, 1995), p. 270. (Wayne) House, "Apostesia," p. 270.

Remember, the Thessalonians had been led astray by the false teaching (2:2-3) that the Day of the Lord had already come. This was confusing because Paul offered great hope, in the first letter, of a departure to be with Christ and a rescue from God's wrath. Now a letter purporting to be from Paul seems to say that they would first have to go through the Day of the Lord. Paul then clarified this prior teaching by emphasizing that they had no need to worry. They could again be comforted because the departure he had discussed in his first letter, and in his teaching while with them, was still the truth. The departure of Christians to be with Christ, and the subsequent revelation of the lawless one, Paul argues, is proof that the Day of the Lord had not begun as they had thought. This understanding of *apostasia* makes much more sense than the view that they are to be comforted (v. 2) because a defection from the faith must precede the Day of the Lord. The entire second chapter (as well as I Thess. 4:18; 5:11) serves to comfort (see v. 2, 3, 17) supplied by a reassurance of Christ's coming as taught in [Paul's] first letter.

Is this translation an accurate rendering of the word, *apostasia*? Given the context it certainly seems to be a reasonable and acceptable rendering. However, as with any doctrine we must be mindful that individual verses confirm a doctrine only when *they collectively reinforce it*. 'One verse does not a doctrine make' without support from several others and general biblical principles. By itself, this argument may not be compelling, but taken together with all of the other biblical references cited in this book it adds additional support to the pre-tribulation and pre-wrath Rapture positions. This verse hardly stands alone as the many verses I include in Chapter 15 demonstrate.

If we agree that the Children of God will not experience God's wrath, then their 'removal' from the earth is necessary before the *Great Tribulation (or the commencement of God's judgments)*. Accordingly, the translation of *apostasia* as 'departure' is, in my opinion, a solid one. It strongly connects to the context of Paul's rationale for writing to the Church at Thessalonica and to the many other passages which together uphold the same truth.

● ● ●

Black Sun, Blood Moon

For Further Reading

Becker, Ernst, *The Denial of Death,* Free Press Paperbacks, New York, 1973, 314 pages.

Busch, David Winston, *The Assyrian: Satan, His Christ, and the Return of the Shadow of Degrees*, Xulon Press, United States, 2007, 339 pages.

Church, J.R., *Daniel Reveals the Blood Line of the Antichrist,* Prophecy Publications, Oklahoma City, OK., 2010, 330 pages.

Custance, Arthur C., *Without Form and Void: A Study of the Meaning of Genesis 1:2*, Classic Reprint Press, Windber, PA., 1970, 275 pages.

Flynn, David, *Temple at the Center of Time: Newton's Bible Codex Deciphered and the Year 2012,*Official Disclosure, A Division of Anomalous Publishing House, Crane, MO., 2008, 296pages.

Heron, Patrick, *The Nephilim and the Pyramid of the Apocalypse,* Citadel Press, Kensington Publishing Corp., New York, 2004, 241pages.

Hitchcock, Mark, *2012: The Bible and the End of the World*, Harvest House Publishers, Eugene, OR., 2009, 184pages.

Horn, Thomas R., *Nephilim Stargates: The Year 2012 and the Return of the Watchers*, Anomalous Publishing House, (Crane, MO.), 2007, 232 pages.

-----------, *Apollyon Rising: 2012*, Anomalous Publishing, Crane, MO., 2009, 352 pages.

Horn, Tom and Nita, *Forbidden Gates,* Defender Publishing Group, Crane, MO., 2011, 350 pages.

James, Terry (Editor), *The Departure: God's Next Catastrophic Intervention into Earth's History,* Defender Publishing, Crane, MO., 2010, 411 pages.

Jeffrey, Grant R., *Countdown to the Apocalypse*, WaterBrook Press (Colorado Springs, Co.), 2008, 227 pages.

-----------, *The New Temple and the Second Coming*, WaterBrook Press, Colorado Springs, 2007, 204 pages.

Lawrence, Joseph E., *Apocalypse 2012: An Investigation into Civilization's End*, Broadway Books (New York), 2007, 2008, 262 pages.

Lowe, David W., *Then His Voice Shook the Earth: Mount Sinai, the Trumpet of God, and the Resurrection of the Dead in Christ*, Seimos Publishing, 2006, 167pages.

Lumpkin, Joseph B., *The Lost Book of Enoch, A Comprehensive Transliteration of the Forgotten Book of the Bible,* Fifth Estate Publishers, Blountsville, AL., 2004, 180 pages.

Montieth, Dr. Stanley, *Brotherhood of Darkness*, Hearthstone Publishing, Oklahoma City, OK., 2010, 144 pages.

Marzulli, L.A., *Politics, Prophecy, and the Supernatural: The Coming Great Deception and the Luciferian Endgame*, Anomalous Publishing, Crane, MO., 2007, 248pages.

Rosenberg, Joel C., *Epicenter 2.0 Version: Updated and Expanded*, Tyndale House Publishers, Carol Stream, IL., 401 pages.

Ryrie, Charles C., *Dispensationalism, Revised and Expanded*, Moody Bible Institute, 2007, 265pages.

Pember, G.H., *Earth's Earliest Ages,* First published by Hodder and Stoughton, London, England, 1876, 380 pages.

Sanger, Mel, *2012: The Year of Project Enoch?* Rema Marketing, London, 2009, 253 pages.

Thomas, I.D.E., *The Omega Conspiracy: Satan's Last Assault on God's Kingdom*, Anomalous Publishing, Crane, MO., 2008, 195 pages.

Woodward, S. Douglas, *Are We Living in the Last D*ays? The Apocalypse Debate in the 21st Century, Faith Happens, Woodinville, WA., 2009, 312 pages.

-------------, *Decoding Doomsday: The 2012 Prophecies, the Apocalypse, and the Perilous Days Ahead,* Defender Publishing Group, Crane, MO., 2010, 380 pages.

About the Author

S. Douglas Woodward ("Doug") is an author and currently an independent consultant serving emerging companies. Over the past twelve years, Doug has served as CEO, COO, and CFO of numerous software and Internet companies. Prior to his tenure in entrepreneurial efforts, he worked as an executive for Honeywell, Oracle, Microsoft, and as a Partner at Ernst & Young LLP. His technical background is in enterprise business strategy, software development and most recently in venture financing and business strategy.

Doug grew up in Oklahoma City, going to high school and college nearby (Norman). At 15, Doug was struck with a serious form of adolescent cancer, *Rhabdomyosarcoma*, which forced him to lose his left leg as a means to treat the disease. At the time of his illness (1969), recovery was likely in less than 10% of the cases diagnosed. The experience had a dramatic impact upon Doug's spiritual life, linking him with dozens of family members, friends, ministers, nurses and doctors who showed great compassion and provided him with remarkable support. Doug cheated death however, through the great efforts of many doctors and the prayers of parents, brothers, family and friends.

Doug attended the University of Oklahoma where he received an Honors Degree in *Letters* (Bachelor of Arts), graduating Cum Laude. His studies focused principally on religious philosophy and theology as well as European history and Latin. In particular, Doug studied under Dr. Tom W. Boyd, a renowned professor, teacher, and speaker there. Doug actively participated in *Young Life* and *Campus Crusade for Christ* throughout his college experience. Upon graduation, Doug served as a Youth Minister and Associate Pastor in the Methodist and Reformed Churches for three years before experimenting with the computer industry as another possible career choice. He grew to love it and has spent thirty-six years in various capacities there. He has written various articles and spoken at many conferences and seminars throughout his career. During his experience at Oracle and Microsoft, much of his efforts were devoted to education and introducing new approaches for better efficiency, making use of distanced learning technologies. Through the years, Doug has served in various capacities in Methodist, Presbyterian, and Reformed Churches. Most recently, Doug served as Elder in the Presbyterian Church.

Doug is married to Donna Wilson Woodward and together they are celebrating thirty-six years of marriage. The Woodward's lived in Oklahoma City until 1987 then moved east. For six years they lived in New England and then have spent the last nineteen years in Woodinville, Washington, a suburb of Seattle. They have two children, Corinne, 32, and Nicholas, 27, and four dogs that are treated far too well.